BOTTLECAPS TO BRUSHES

Art Activities for Kids

From the National Museum of American Art

LYNN-STEVEN ENGELKE

Cappy illustrations by
LYNN PUTNEY

NATIONAL MUSEUM OF AMERICAN ART

Smithsonian Institution

This publication is made possible with the generous support of the James Smithson Society.

*"I used to draw like Raphael, but it has taken me a
whole lifetime to learn to draw like children."*—Picasso
For my students at Glenelg Country School

To Brita, Chris, Cindy, David, Jill, Lark, Lynn,
Meggan, Melissa, Phil, Robert, Sally, and Steve—
for their energy, creativity, and guidance.
Lynn-Steven Engelke

Printed in Hong Kong.

Chief of Publications and New Media Initiatives: Steve Dietz
Editor: Melissa Hirsch
Editorial Assistant: Abigail Grotke
Art Director: Lynn-Steven Engelke
Museum Education Consultant: Sally Hoffmann
Activities Editor: Kimberly Cody
Designer: Robert Killian
Cappy illustrations: Lynn Putney
Cover Design: Steve Bell

ISBN 0-937311-28-6

Library of Congress Cataloging-in-Publication Data
    Engelke, Lynn-Steven.
Bottle caps to brushes : art activities for kids / Lynn-Steven Engelke.
        p.   cm.
    Summary: A cartoon giraffe based on a sculpture at the National
Museum of American Art gives a tour of some of the museum's
exhibits and offers activities showing how to create various types of art
using everyday materials.
    ISBN 0-937311-28-6
    1. Art appreciation—Juvenile literature. 2. Activity programs in
education—Juvenile literature. [1. National Museum of American Art
(U.S.)—Exhibitions. 2. Art, American—Exhibitions. 3. Art apprecia-
tion. 4. Art—Technique.] I. National Museum of American Art (U.S.)
II. Title.
N7477.E5 1995
701'.1—dc20   95-4410   CIP   AC

The National Museum of American Art, Smithsonian Institution, is dedicated to
the preservation, exhibition, and study of the visual arts in America. Its publications program includes the scholarly journal *American Art*. The museum also
has extensive research resources: the databases of the Inventories of American
Art, several image archives, and a variety of fellowships for scholars. The
Renwick Gallery, one of the premier crafts museums, is part of NMAA. For
more information or a catalogue of publications, write: Office of Publications,
MRC-210, National Museum of American Art, Smithsonian Institution,
Washington, D.C. 20560. NMAA also maintains a gopher site at **nmaa-
ryder.si.edu** and a World Wide Web site at **http://nmaa.si.edu**. For further
information, send e-mail to **NMAA.NMAAInfo@ic.si.edu**.

MEET CAPPY!   4

GET THE PICTURE!   8
Art makes a record of what you see.

WHAT'S THE STORY?   17
Art shares a story.

ZOOM OUT! ZOOM IN!   24
Art gives different ways of seeing.

SEEING RED? FEELING BLUE?   33
Art uses color to show many moods.

DON'T THROW THAT AWAY!   40
Art uses everyday items in unusual ways.

CAN YOU FIND THE SECRET MESSAGE?   49
Art plays with letters and numbers.

DO YOU KNOW WHAT I THINK?   60
Art shows your point of view.

SURPRISE US!   69
Art makes something that's never been made before.

CAPPY SAYS GOOD-BYE!   76

MEET CAPPY!

Do these three bottle caps make you think about giraffes? Probably not. But you haven't met **me** yet.

My name is Cappy, and I'm a skateboarding giraffe. I'm a cartoon character based on a bottle cap sculpture at the National Museum of American Art. I live here, and I'll be showing you some of the other works of art in the museum's collection.

Look at the sculpture in this picture. How is it like a real giraffe? How is it different?

Unidentified Artist, *Bottlecap Giraffe* (detail)

You've seen giraffes in the zoo, and I'll bet you can draw a pretty good picture of one. Would your drawing look anything like this sculpture?

If you look at the sculpture closely, you'll notice that where real giraffes have spotted fur, this giraffe has hundreds of bottle caps. The artist who made him saved the tops from bottles that were made in France, Canada, and the United States. He used them in a new way . . . to cover his giraffe. Then he put his sculpture on wheels.

Now look at **me**. How am I different?

The cartoonist who made me had a different idea. She couldn't put bottle caps in a book, so she used a hole punch and decorated paper to make my colorful spots. And she gave me a skateboard!

Unidentified Artist,
Bottlecap Lion

You see, artists don't only use brushes and paint. Art can be made with crayons, or colored paper, or old socks, or dried flowers or . . . bottle caps! The possibilities are endless. There is no limit to an artist's imagination — or yours.

Now that you've met me, some of your ideas about art have changed, haven't they?

National Museum of American Art, Smithsonian Institution

This happens all the time when you look at a work of art. That's what artists want to happen. They want to give you a new way to see the world and new ideas about the way you live in it.

They might even want to give you new ideas about giraffes!

I usually stand near the front door, welcoming visitors. But sometimes, when things aren't too busy, I jump on my

Now, let's see what we can find!

skateboard and look around. I always find something new to see and think about.

Sometimes I try out these new ideas. But what I create in my artwork is unique — it could only come from me! The same is true of you.

Shall I show you some of my favorite works of art in the museum?

When we get to my favorite artists, we'll read about them together. Then I'll tell you about the art I've made using some of their ideas, so you can try it, too.

And since you don't know your way around the museum as well as I do, I'll show you the way.

Wherever I go, I see something that would make a good picture.

What I see might seem pretty ordinary, but the pictures I make sure aren't!

And I don't even need a camera to take them!

Every time I look at something, my eyes are like the lens of a camera. When I think about whether what I see would make a good picture or not, my imagination is my viewfinder. How do I "develop" my pictures? With crayons, paint, clay . . . sometimes even film.

Making pictures is one way to remember things, and to share your thoughts and memories with other people, too. By recording what you see, you show them how the world looks through **your** eyes and from **your** point of view.

What do you think artists in this museum are showing us in their artwork?

Let's find out!

But before we go, watch this!

(opposite) Alvan Fisher, *A General View of the Falls of Niagara* (detail)

Wouldn't I make a great picture?

LARRY YÁÑEZ
(b. 1949)

Larry Yáñez, *Cocina Jaiteca, from the National Chicano Screenprint Taller, 1988–1989*

"Look around your own world!"

If you need ideas for art, that's what Larry Yáñez says you should do.

That's how he gets **his** ideas. He looks around his world, and then he puts what he sees into his art.

Larry Yáñez's world is a fascinating one. He grew up in the Southwest, and he enjoys being part of the Chicano community there. In his community and in his art-work, the customs of the United States and Mexico are combined.

He says that he likes to throw "snatches" and "clashes" of things together. Memories from his childhood and scenes of everyday life now — he puts them all in his art.

That's what he did when he made *Cocina Jaiteca*. It looks like a picture of a kitchen. But it's really a picture of **many** kitchens.

When Larry Yáñez was young, he would often spend afternoons at his aunts' houses. He would push his toy cars and trucks around under their kitchen tables and listen to his mother and her sisters talk. When he looked up from where he was sitting, everything in the room seemed large and a little oddly shaped. In his memories, all of these afternoons and all of these kitchens have been jumbled. So that's how he made *Cocina Jaiteca* — it's a jumble of kitchens, all mixed together, as seen from the floor.

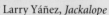

Larry Yáñez, *Jackalope*

JACKALOPE

A lot of the titles Larry Yáñez gives to his artwork are "Spanglish," a mixture of English and Spanish. *Cocina Jaiteca,* for example, is a play on words. In Spanish, *cocina* means kitchen. *Jaiteca* is a made-up word. But because in Spanish the "j" is pronounced like an "h," *jaiteca* also sounds like "high tech." Does the *cocina* in the painting look "high tech" and up-to-date? Or does it look *jaiteca*?

SELF

Larry Yáñez, *Self*

Why did he decide to make a picture of something as ordinary as a kitchen? We all know what kitchens are like; we see them all the time.

That's exactly why Larry Yáñez chose it. He knows that we usually don't pay much attention to what we see everyday, but that doesn't mean these things aren't important. Ordinary things help us imagine the daily lives of the people who use them.

So Larry Yáñez isn't just letting us see a kitchen through his eyes.

He's helping us to take a look around his whole world!

COULD YOU GUESS THAT . . .

. . . Larry Yáñez is a Jackalope? A *jackalope* is an imaginary animal that's part jack rabbit and part antelope. It's also the name of a music group! Larry Yáñez and his friends play in a band called the Jackalopes. Their music mixes different instruments and rhythms in exciting new ways. Like the *jackalope,* they join things together to make something fantastic!

. . . *Cocina Jaiteca* is not a painting? It was printed in ink on paper, using a method called silkscreen. *Cocina Jaiteca* has twelve different colors in it. Can you find them? (If you need a hint, remember that the paper is white.)

. . . Larry Yáñez loved typewriters? When he was a little boy, it took a long time for him to write his letters. But with this machine he could print them over and over again, always perfectly. Now he uses printmaking methods, like silkscreen, to make his art.

. . . you can walk around inside of some of Larry Yáñez's artwork? Some of his sculptures fill whole rooms, and he says they're like "giant postcards" of the world he wants us to see.

ACTIVITIES THAT MAKE A RECORD OF WHAT YOU SEE

"Life is painting a picture, not doing a sum."

—*Oliver Wendell Holmes*

HOME SWEET HOME

Larry Yáñez likes recording all the details that show what a Chicano home looks like. Besides the kitchen, he's already made pictures of a living room, called "Sofa, So Good" (**another** play on words!) and a bathroom. Soon he'll add a bedroom, a garage, and a garden. If he puts them all together, he'll have a whole house!

I had fun making the rooms in **my** house, too. Now, even if someone can't come to visit me, I can still show them what I see when I skate through the museum.

Since I live in a museum, my home is probably very different from yours. Let's see, there's the gallery, the cafeteria . . .

This is how to make your house:

1. Get out these supplies:
   - construction paper (9" x 12" sheets)
   - pencil
   - scissors
   - glue
   - stiff brush for glue
   - markers, crayons, or colored pencils

2. Make your rooms.

- Fold each sheet of paper in half, then cut along the fold line.
- Use one half-sheet of paper for each room.
- With your ruler and pencil, draw a guideline on the left-hand edge of each sheet of paper. (Use the width of your ruler to measure.)
- Fold each sheet along the guideline. You've just made glue tabs!

3. Turn your rooms into a house.

- Line your sheets of paper up in a row.
- Let the right-hand edge of each sheet overlap the glue tab on the next one.
- Glue the papers together, making sure the edges line up with the guidelines. Use the paintbrush to spread the glue evenly, and make sure not to use too much glue — it might bleed through the paper.
- Now put your house together. Fold the paper rooms back and forth along their edges, like a big fan.
- Open your house up. It will be like a zig-zag, but it will stand up by itself.

4. Fill your rooms.

- Make every sheet of paper into a different room.
- Use your markers, crayons, or colored pencils to draw everything that might be in each room, including doors and windows.
- You can draw make-believe rooms or the rooms in your own house.

5. Move into your house.

- Who will live in your house? Use another sheet of construction paper to make paper characters. You can make yourself, your pet, or anybody you'd like to share your house.

6. If you and a friend make these houses together, you can trade them. That way, you'll have a whole new way to "visit" each other!

Joseph E. Yoakum, *Art Linkletter's Ranch near Darwin, Australia*

WISH YOU WERE HERE!

While Larry Yáñez makes pictures of the world he sees everyday, Joseph E. Yoakum made drawings of a world he may never have seen at all! **He worked from his imagination.**

He told amazing stories about leaving his family's home on a Navajo reservation and going all over the world. He described traveling with a circus, in the army, and on a boat. There are "few places I haven't been, of any size that is. And there's nothing I haven't suffered to see things first hand," he said.

This might have all been **make believe**, so his drawings are a little like souvenirs or postcards from places he has never visited.

They certainly look like **official** souvenirs! He always signed them (sometimes including his zip code and a rubber stamp to show the date), and he wrote an exact name for the place he said he visited.

Do you think it matters if he was ever really there or not? Sometimes you have a lot to say about places you can only imagine.

What places would you like to visit?

Will you send a postcard?

1. **Get out these supplies:**
   - pencils (#2 and colored)
   - scrap paper
   - lightweight posterboard (4" x 6")
   - scissors (or pinking shears)
   - ruler
   - black felt-tip pen
   - tissue

2. **Where are you?**
   - You can pretend you're sending your card from anywhere — the playground down the street, or a city on the moon!
   - Will you put the name of your vacation spot on the front of the card? Yoakum always did!

3. **Make your postcard.**
   - Use a pencil to draw the outlines of your picture on your posterboard.
   - Go over your pencil lines with pen.
   - Fill in your shapes with colored pencil.
   - Try rubbing the colored pencil lines with tissue paper. This is what Yoakum did to make his pictures look like softly colored watercolors.

   - Lots of postcards have zig-zag edges. Use scissors or pinking shears to cut the sides of yours.

4. **Write your message.**
   - On the other side of your postcard, use your pen and ruler to divide your postcard into two sections.
   - Who do you want to read your message? Put a name and address on the right-hand side of your card.
   - What do you want to say? Write one or two sentences about your real or imaginary place on the left-hand side of the card.

5. **Mail your postcard!**
   - Even if you're just pretending to send your postcard, you need a pretend stamp! Don't forget the postmark!

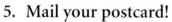

Activity Two

DO YOU SEE WHAT I SEE?

All of these pictures show Niagara Falls, a famous waterfall on the New York/Canadian border. When they looked at the falls, each of these artists saw something very different. That's what happens in art. We get to show — and see — the world from different points of view!

Barbara Bosworth, *Niagara Falls*

John Henry Twachtman, *Niagara Falls*

George Inness, *Niagara Falls*

1. **Get out these supplies:**
   - drawing paper (one large sheet and several small sheets)
   - street map or newspaper from your area
   - your favorite art supplies (markers, crayons, paints, etc.)
   - scissors
   - ruler
   - pencil
   - tape or glue

2. **Pick a scene.**
   - Look around your yard, your street, and your neighborhood.
   - A *landscape* picture is always of the outdoors.
   - You don't have to find a nature scene, or even a "pretty" one. Pictures of buildings make a good "cityscape." And anything you see around you can make a good picture!

3. **Choose your views.**
   - If you're working with your friends, sit close together. That way, you'll all be looking at the same scene, but you'll each have your own point of view.
   - If you're working alone, plan to make your picture two or three times, each time from a different angle.

4. **Make your pictures.**
   - Use the small pieces of drawing paper.
   - Let everyone choose their favorite art supplies.
   - If you're making more than one picture, use different supplies for each one.
   - Your picture should fill the paper.

5. **Put your views together.**
   - Cover the large sheet of paper with your neighborhood map or newspaper.
   - Cut openings to make windows for your different views.
   - Glue or tape each view behind its window. You don't need to show the whole picture!

6. **Enjoy your differences!**
   - With all these views together, we can really "get the picture!"

Activity Three

WHAT'S THE STORY?

Art does more than just show what you see.

It tells about events you **remember** and stories you've heard.

Some of these stories are very **private and personal**. But sometimes art tells the story of a **whole group of people**.

It can even tell the story of a whole group of animals!

How we giraffes learned to eat from treetops is an especially fascinating story.

Do you think I could turn it into an art project?

There are a lot of wonderful stories in the artwork here in my museum.

So, before I get out my art supplies again, let's find some of them.

(opposite) Jacob Lawrence, *Men Exist for the Sake of One Another. Teach Them Then or Bear with Them (from the Great Ideas of Western Man series)* (detail)

VELINO SHIJE HERRERA

(1902 – 1973)

There are three stories **hidden** in this painting.

Can you find them?

The first one is easy to see.

Nine children are sitting quietly, making part of a circle. The tenth child is standing up. His hand is behind an old man who's sitting with them. He could be their grandfather, or he might be a **teacher**. From the way the children are watching him, we can guess that he must be telling them something important!

Velino Shije Herrera, *Story Teller* (detail)

If you read the title of the painting, you know the **children are hearing a story.** But that's just one of the stories in the painting!

The second story is a little harder to see.

Did you notice that four of the children are wearing Native American clothing, and that they're all looking at the story teller with respect? That's because, in Native American communities, the storyteller has a very serious job. While he's telling the children stories, he's also teaching them lessons — where their people came from, what they've learned about raising plants and animals, what they believe, and how to behave. This is how the story teller passes his community's way of life from the older people to the younger ones.

The **storyteller's job** is the second story we can see in this painting. What do you think the third story could be?

This story is the hardest one to see. It's the story of how this painting came to be made.

The artist who painted *Story Teller* was named Velino Shije Herrera. He was a Pueblo Indian. Pueblo is the Spanish word for town or village. For years and years, the towns the Pueblo people lived in didn't change very much, and the **way** they lived in them didn't change much either. They sang the same songs, danced the same dances, and told the same stories that they always had.

That's what Velino Herrera wanted to put in his paintings — all the **customs of Pueblo life** that hadn't changed since before he was born.

But some things had changed, and one of them was the way the Pueblo Indian artists painted.

New Mexico state flag

Long ago, **Native American artists** didn't use water-color, and they certainly never had gouache — the special kind of watercolor Velino Herrera used to paint *Story Teller.* He learned to use gouache in school, during art classes set up by the government. The teachers in these classes showed their students new kinds of art supplies. Later, Velino Herrera worked in one of these schools himself, teaching this new style of painting to other young Native Americans.

So the third story in this painting is the story of how Native American art changed with the introduction of new materials.

Now you've seen the **stories hidden in the painting**. By themselves, each story is interesting. But, really, all three stories are connected.

Doesn't that make them even more interesting?

And doesn't that make the painting more interesting, too?

COULD YOU GUESS THAT . . .

. . . Velino Herrera's friends called him the "singing artist," **because he was always singing as he painted?** Singing reminds us of birds, and Velino Herrera was also named for a bird. His Indian-language name was Ma Pe Wi, which means red bird or oriole.

. . . **the New Mexico state flag (left) has one of Velino Herrera's designs on it?** Zia, the name of his pueblo, is also the Indian-language symbol for sun. Velino Herrera gave his version of the Zia symbol to the state government, and they made it the official state seal. Now you can see it all over New Mexico — even on the license plates!

. . . **a lot of people in the Zia community didn't think Velino Herrera should have given the Zia sign away?** They thought only the Pueblo people should be able to use it. What do you think?

. . . **Pueblo potters often make story teller figures out of clay?** These clay figures are usually shown holding children, because children love their stories. They usually have their mouths open, too, because they love to talk!

Awa Tsireh, *Black Mountain Lion and Black Fox* (details)

ACTIVITIES THAT SHARE A STORY

"One picture is worth more than a thousand words."

—*Chinese proverb*

A BEDTIME STORY

I like hearing stories anytime, but I especially like them at bedtime. I like to snuggle down in my quilt while I'm listening. Even if I fall asleep, the stories are still important to me. They get all mixed up in my dreams!

I've made a picture about my cozy story time. Here's how I did it:

1. **Get out these supplies:**
   - fabric scraps
   - scissors
   - drawing paper (a large sheet)
   - pencil
   - glue
   - stiff brush for glue
   - markers

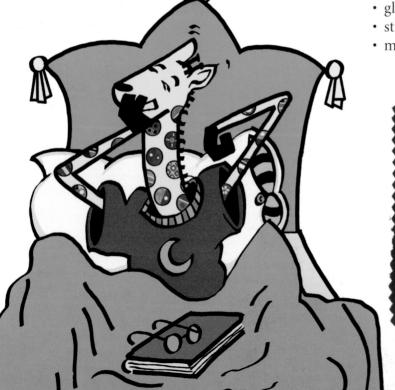

2. **"Sew" a quilt.**
   - Cut the fabric scraps into small squares (each one about the size of a postage stamp). The more patterns you use, the better!
   - Use your pencil to make the outline of a rectangle on your drawing paper.
   - Fit your fabric squares together inside this rectangle. Trim or add pieces to make the shape even.
   - Move the patches so you can glue them to the drawing paper. Use your paintbrush to spread a thin layer of glue inside the rectangle. Then, fill the rectangle with your fabric squares, making sure they line up side-by-side. (You don't want a hole in your quilt!)

3. **Tuck yourself into bed.**
   - Using your markers, draw your room, your bed, and yourself!

4. **Tell yourself a story.**
   - Will you be reading your favorite book, or will you be dreaming?

Activity Four

A T-SHIRT QUILT

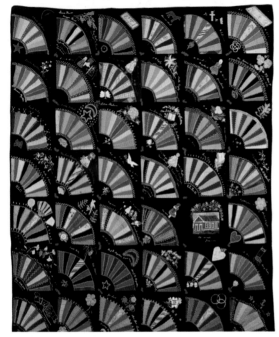

Residents of Bourbon County, Kentucky,
Fan Quilt, Mt. Carmel

Do you have a lot of outgrown T-shirts? I sure do. I even have my first T-shirt from the museum! Opening my dresser drawer is like opening a scrapbook! I just can't throw any of these memories away.

When I was working on my "Bedtime Story" project, I noticed the Bourbon County quilt here at my museum. It's a friendship quilt, which means that a lot of people made it — probably as a present for a friend. They wanted

their friend to remember them, so they put reminders in every square. By including a picture of their church and the names of all one hundred and ten members, the quilters sewed a sort of story about their lives into their quilt.

I decided to let my old T-shirts tell a story about **my** life. Here's how I did it:

1. **Ask an adult for help.**
   • Make sure it's okay to use your old shirts and the iron.

2. **Get out these supplies:**
   • old T-shirts
   • an old pillowcase
   • scissors or pinking shears
   • fusible webbing (This is an iron-on fabric adhesive that you can get at most craft or fabric stores. You will need a piece about the same size as your T-shirt.)
   • iron
   • permanent-ink pen

Activity Five

3. **Get ready to "sew!"**
   • Your pillowcase will be the quilt backing.
   • Choose the T-shirts that bring back the most memories.
   • Is everything clean and pressed?
   • Cut out the interesting names and pictures printed on your T-shirts.

4. **Make your design.**
   • Spread all your T-shirt cut-outs on the floor.
   • How do they fit together? This is like a puzzle, only you're using fabric.
   • Look at your arrangement. Move your T-shirt pieces around to find the pattern you like best.
   • Trim your pieces so the edges line up.

5. **Put your quilt together.**
   • Set your quilt pieces on your pillowcase.
   • Are the pieces just where you want them? Do they fit together well?
   • Read the instructions that come with the fusible webbing.
   • Ask an adult to help you attach the quilt pieces to the backing. It's less confusing if you work on just one quilt piece at a time!

6. **Share your story.**
   • With your pen, add names and dates to some of your pieces.
   • Now everyone can "read" about you in your quilt.

DEAR DIARY

Telling and listening to stories is fun. Sometimes I feel like I'm the museum's Story Teller, because I have so much to tell the visitors!

When we go on a tour of the museum, I feel a little like the museum's quilt maker, too. Each piece of artwork is different from every other piece, but we can find ways they fit together, too.

Some artwork fits together because the artists have chosen the same subject or theme for their work. In their art, they're telling us similar stories!

Artists Roger Shimomura and Jack Earl both show someone reading or writing. What do you think **their** stories are about? I know there's a letter and a journal, but I wish I knew more!

I decided to make a journal of my own. Here's what I did:

1. **Get out these supplies:**
   - several sheets of paper
   - lightweight posterboard (two pieces, slightly larger than the paper)
   - pencils (#2 and colored) and markers
   - ruler
   - hole punch
   - a strong rubber band (Colored ones look especially nice.)
   - a fairly straight, sturdy rod, no longer than your cardboard (A tongue depressor, a heavy twig, or even two popsicle sticks glued together will all work well. What else could you use?)

2. **Make your pages.**
   - You can use different textures and colors of paper.
   - Stack your pages in the order you want them.

3. **Cover your book.**
   - Put your stack of pages between the two cardboard covers like a sandwich.
   - Make sure all the edges are even.
   - How will your book open? Most books open from the right-hand side. I like my sketchbooks to open from the bottom.

4. **Pull it all together.**
   - Use your pencil and ruler to draw two small "*X*'s" on the binding edge of your front cover (the edge opposite from the side you want to open).

Roger Shimomura, *Diary: December 12, 1941*

The "*X*'s" should be 1/4" from the binding edge and at least 1" from the top and bottom of the cover.
- Punch two holes in the cover where you made the "*X*'s".
- Using the holes in your cover as a guide, punch holes in the same places on all the pages and on the back cover. Keep everything in order!
- Holding your book together, place the rod along the binding edge of the front cover. Loop one end of the rubberband around the rod. Push the other end of the rubber band through all the top holes of your book, then pull it back through all the bottom holes. Loop it around the bottom of the rod. Open your book!

5. **What story will you tell us?**
   - Your journal can be a place to draw or write about your dreams, your plans, or just what you did during the day.
   - Decorate your cover to show us what will be in your book.

Jack Earl, *Dear Fay . . .*

Activity Six

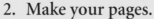

Gus Foster, *Cut Wheat*

ZOOM OUT!

Thomas Hart Benton, *Wheat* (detail)

ZOOM IN!

Have you ever looked at a plant through a magnifying glass?

Before I had, I thought I knew what stems and leaves looked like. When I look out of the big windows in the museum, I can see lots of them.

But the view I have through the museum windows is nothing like the one I have through my magnifying glass!

When you look at something in a new way, it can seem completely different. You might not even recognize it at first.

When you **do** recognize it, though, you understand what you're seeing in a new way, too.

You see it from a different point of view.

I've been wondering how my museum looks to people visiting it for the first time.

From the outside, it might not seem as big as it does to me. But it's big enough to hold more than 37,500 works of art!

And a lot of this artwork gives us different ways of looking at things.

So get ready to see something new — even if I'm **not** bringing my magnifying glass!

GEORGIA O'KEEFFE
(1887 – 1986)

Even when she was a baby, Georgia O'Keeffe saw the world around her a little differently than most people do. Can you describe anything that you saw before you were a year old? Georgia O'Keeffe could. The shapes and patterns on a quilt she played on before she could even stand up were still clear to her almost eighty years later!

When Georgia O'Keeffe was growing up, most girls learned embroidery and other sorts of artwork that help decorate a house. Some girls became art teachers. But very few girls were encouraged to try to make their livings as artists! O'Keeffe didn't see things that way at all. She started taking art lessons, and when she was twelve years old, she decided to become an artist.

One day, in her high school art class, she experimented with a new way of looking at the world. Holding up a wildflower, her teacher showed how important it was for her to examine it carefully before drawing it. O'Keeffe did look at it closely, but she did a lot more than that. She turned it in different directions, drawing it over and over again. Then she tried drawing just a part of it, to see what that would look like. Every time she drew it, she made the shape of the flower look more simple. Someone looking at her drawing might not have recognized the flower at all. That didn't matter to Georgia O'Keeffe. To her, just to copy the flower was dull. In her drawings, a flower became a world to be explored.

After she'd been painting for a few years, O'Keeffe realized that she'd begun copying other artists. But she still didn't see things

"This abominable machine will be the death of me yet."

Georgia O'Keeffe, drawn for her high school yearbook, *The Mortar Board*

the same way they did, so her paintings disappointed her. Then she remembered what she'd learned in her high school art class.

For the rest of her life, she was determined to paint what she saw in her **own** way. Because her way was so unusual, her artwork sometimes startles us. That would please Georgia O'Keeffe, because that's what she wanted to happen. She said she wanted people to be "surprised into taking time to look . . . to see what I see of flowers."

Can you see her point of view?

Georgia O'Keeffe, drawn for her high school yearbook, *The Mortar Board*

Georgia O'Keeffe, *Only One*

COULD YOU GUESS THAT . . .

. . . Georgia O'Keeffe disliked it when people called her a "woman artist?" She didn't think that being a woman should matter to her art. She wanted to be thought of only as **"an** artist."

. . . she drew cartoons of her teachers for her high school yearbook? She was the art editor, and her classmates put this rhyme under her picture:

> *O is for O'Keeffe; an artist divine*
> *Her paintings are perfect and her drawings are fine.*

. . . In 1977, Georgia O'Keeffe received the U.S. Medal of Freedom? This is the highest honor our government gives to a civilian.

. . . she didn't sign her paintings? She didn't think she had to — she thought people would be able to tell they were hers because of what she painted and how she painted it. Do you think you could recognize one of her paintings?

. . . Georgia O'Keeffe lived and painted on her ranch in New Mexico until she was almost one hundred years old? Where else in this book have you seen art from the Southwest?

ACTIVITIES THAT GIVE DIFFERENT WAYS OF SEEING THINGS

"Where the telescope ends, the microscope begins. Which of the two has the grander view?"

—*Victor Hugo*

A CLOSER VIEW

When you looked at Georgia O'Keeffe's paintings, could you tell right away what they were? It might have been a little hard at first. Sometimes she liked to focus on just a small part of whatever she was painting, and sometimes she made a single object fill the whole frame. A close-up view like that could fool anybody!

This is the way I "zoom-in" when I want to make a close-up picture. Do you think I could fool you?

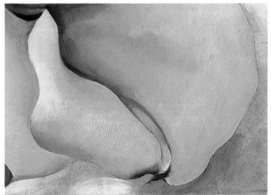

(detail)

Here's what I **do:**

1. **Get out these supplies:**
   - lightweight cardboard (one 6" x 6" square)
   - ruler
   - pencil
   - scissors
   - two paper clips
   - drawing paper
   - paintbrush
   - watercolors
   - jar of water
   - rag or paper towel

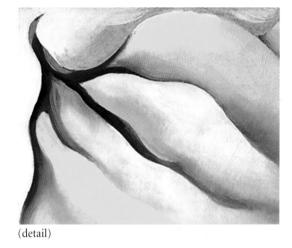

(detail)

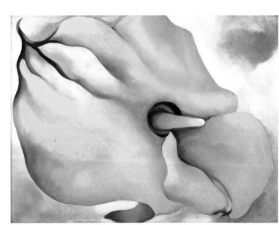

Georgia O'Keeffe, *Yellow Calla*

Where would you have to be standing to see a real flower look this big? That would be **your** point of view!

3. Try out different views.

- Look at this book through your viewfinder. "Zoom out" by moving the viewfinder closer to your eye. What do you see? (Try not to pay attention to anything outside of your frame!) You probably see the whole book and part of the room around it. Now, "zoom in" by moving the viewfinder closer to the page. Do you see much more than a few words?

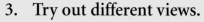

Activity Seven

2. Make a viewfinder.

- With your pencil and ruler, draw two L-shapes along the edges of your cardboard. The width of your ruler is a good measurement to use.
- Cut the L-shapes out. Now you have two halves of a frame. You won't need the small square that's left over.
- Hold the shapes together to make a whole frame. What shapes can it become? What sizes? Experiment!
- Use your paper clips to join the L's together in a viewfinder shape you like.

4. "Focus" your picture.

- Use your viewfinder to search the room. What would make an interesting picture?
- "Zoom in!" If you move your viewfinder close enough, you'll only be able to see simple shapes, colors, and patterns.

5. Make your close-up picture.

- Hold your viewfinder very still.
- Pretend the viewfinder is the frame of your picture. This means you shouldn't add anything you don't see inside of it.
- With your pencil and paper, draw the outline of everything you see inside your viewfinder. Fill your paper, and don't forget the details!
- Use watercolors to make your picture colorful. Be sure to clean your brush with water before you dip it in a new color. (Georgia O'Keeffe was famous for working with a very clean palette, or color-mixing tray. That's why the colors in her paintings are so clear.)

6. Ask a friend to give your picture a title.

- Could they recognize your close-up view?

THE INSIDE STORY!

There are monkeys hiding in this jungle. Can you find them?

What else do you see hidden inside this picture?

To Alfredo Arreguín, a walk in the jungle is a real adventure. There are so many unexpected sights, and they don't always make sense—a little like a dream. The longer and deeper you look, the more you see.

Alfredo Arreguín, *Sueño (Dream: Eve Before Adam)* (detail)

Arreguín wanted to show all this in his painting. He thought about the shapes, colors and patterns of real plants and animals and crowded his picture with them. When he added the monkeys, he gave them the same designs. They blended right in! When this happens in nature, it's called camouflage. Camouflage helps animals hide from other animals, and from each other. In art, it's used to trick you a little, to make you see things in a new way.

I'd like to have a picture like this one as a camouflage for me. Can you draw one? When visitors come to the museum, they'll think I've disappeared! But to really fool people, the picture has to have a lot of detail. To see me, they might have to turn the page in different directions, hold it up close, or stand back from it a little. If you can draw a good hiding place, send it to me at the museum.* I'd like to try it out.

Mail your drawing to Cappy, c/o the National Museum of American Art, Smithsonian Institution, Washington, D.C. 20560.

THE BIG PICTURE

Shown up close and from very far away, wheat looks very different in these three pictures.

When we look at them lined up together, it almost seems as if we're focusing in on the plant through the zoom lens of a camera.

It's fun to make your own close-up pictures, and it's even more fun to see if your friends can guess what they are.

See who can fill in "the big picture!"

Here's what to do:

1. **Get out these supplies:**
   - old magazines
   - scissors
   - two sheets of drawing paper
   - glue
   - a small jar lid
   - pencil
   - stapler
   - markers

Gus Foster, *Cut Wheat*

Joe Jones, *Men and Wheat*

Thomas Hart Benton, *Wheat*

2. **Find your "big picture."**
   - Look through the magazines and choose a picture you like. A colored photograph that covers the whole page works best.
   - Cut your picture from the magazine and glue it to one sheet of your drawing paper.

3. **Make a "zoom-in" frame.**
   - What is the most interesting part of your picture? "Zoom in" on a detail that's a little hard to recognize.
   - Put your second piece of drawing paper on top of your picture.

With your pencil, mark an "X" over the interesting area.
   - Put the jar lid over the "X." Use your pencil to draw around it. This circle will be the opening of your frame.
   - Cut out the circle and throw it away.
   - Put the frame on top of your picture. Make sure you can see your interesting area through it.
   - Staple the papers together on all four corners.

4. **"Zoom-out."**
   - Show your "zoom-in" picture to your friends. What do they think is hidden by the frame?
   - Ask them to use the markers to draw the missing part of the picture on the frame.

5. **Now take a second look.**
   - Remove the staples and lift up the frame. Did your friends guess what was in the "big picture"?

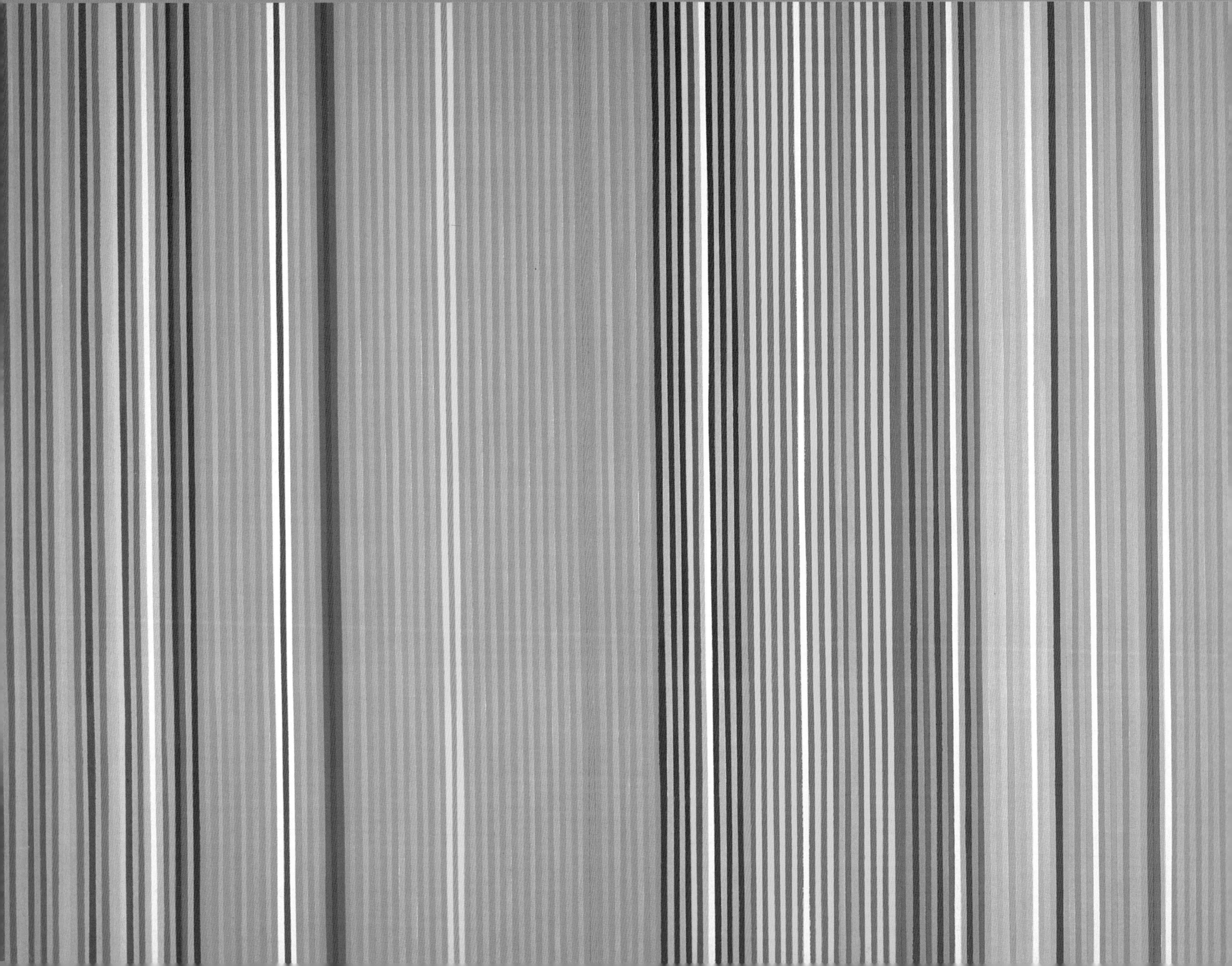

SEEING RED? FEELING BLUE?

Some artists **use color like a language**, to say things that aren't easy to say in words.

Do colors have meanings for you?

They do for me!

This painting always makes me think of a family picnic. The colors remind me of the summer fruit we pack in our basket and the grassy slope where we spread our blanket. **The painting looks warm and happy to me.**

Gene Davis, *Raspberry Icicle*

But what if the artist had made all the green stripes darker? And what if he hadn't used yellow at all?

How would the picture make you feel, then?

You can put your feelings in your artwork. The colors you pick can help you.

That's what our next group of artists did.

What *do* the colors in their artwork mean to you?

ALMA THOMAS
(1891 – 1978)

Do the **trees** near your house **play music?**

Do the **flowers** in your neighborhood **sing and dance?**

When Alma Thomas looked at her garden, she imagined that sometimes they did.

When the wind blew through the trees in her yard, she heard the leaves hum. When the sun was bright, she watched the flowers turn to face the sky.

Although she lived in the same small house in Washington, D.C. for almost her entire life, **she watched her garden change every day.** Some of the changes were small ones — the grass looked greener after a spring rain, and the leaves began to change color after the first fall frost. But some of the changes were much bigger — a fall storm knocked branches and blossoms to the ground, and once the moon moved in front of the sun in an eclipse, making the shadows sharper and colors deeper than usual.

Alma Thomas **enjoyed all of these changes.** They made her garden more interesting to her. And they

Alma Thomas in her studio

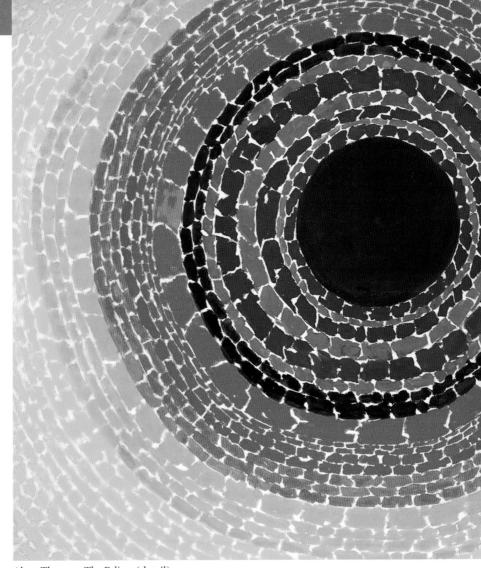

Alma Thomas, *The Eclipse* (detail)

made her think about ways she could change her paintings, to make them just as interesting as her garden.

She wanted to try **a new kind of painting** — unlike anything she'd ever seen or done before. But how? As she thought about this, she stood at her window, watching the holly tree in her front yard. She decided to try painting

COULD YOU GUESS THAT . . .

. . . Alma Thomas often did artwork with children? She worked as an art teacher in city schools. She loved teaching, but she also loved learning — especially the new lessons she discovered in her students' art.

. . . her first summers were spent on her grandfather's farm in Alabama? She had birds and animals to play with, wildflowers and cotton to pick, and colored clay from the brook to make into little cups and plates. When she started painting, she remembered these happy months and began "painting nature."

. . . she was excited about new discoveries in science and technology? She was especially interested in the space program. Photographs taken from satellites gave her new ways to see the world, and she often painted from them.

. . . the people in her neighborhood in Washington, D.C. had many problems and hardships? She said that her paintings show that people can be "living in the heart of the ghetto and seeing beauty."

. . . Alma Thomas was known for smiling at everyone she met? She was cheerful and encouraging — in her artwork and in person!

everything she saw — the sun shining through the leaves, the breeze rustling them, the shadows changing their shape and color. This would be her **new kind of painting!**

"I got some watercolors and some crayons, and I began dabbling," she said. "Little dabs of color that spread out very free . . . that's how it all began. And every morning since then, the wind has given me **new colors through the windowpanes.**"

Alma Thomas put these new colors and patterns into her paintings to show us the kinds of changes she enjoyed watching. Then, when she was finished, she gave her paintings special names, to tell us what they reminded her of and why they made her happy.

The titles Alma Thomas chose for her paintings tell us that the wind brought her much more than new colors to paint. It made her crepe myrtle tree seem to play music and the flowers on her azalea bush **sing and dance** to rock 'n' roll!

Alma Thomas, *Autumn Leaves Fluttering in the Breeze*

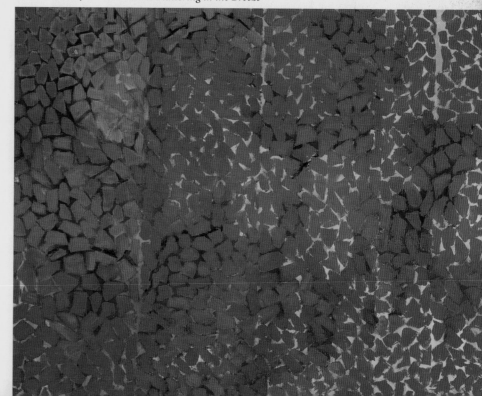

ACTIVITIES THAT USE COLOR TO EXPRESS MOODS

"Colors seen by candlelight will not look the same by day."
—*Elizabeth Barrett Browning*

A LEAF CONCERT

After I learned about Alma Thomas's dancing leaves, I noticed how much the trees outside the museum move in the wind. They have a lot of natural rhythm. All they need is the music. So let's give them a band of leaf musicians!

1. **Get out these supplies:**
    - drawing paper (a large sheet of newsprint, manila, or any other fairly absorbent paper)
    - scrap paper
    - paintbrush
    - watercolors
    - jar of water
    - paper towels
    - markers

(opposite) Alma Thomas, *Red Azaleas Singing and Dancing Rock and Roll Music* (detail)

2. **Look for leaves.**
    - Collect them from trees, bushes, flowers . . . even weeds!
    - If they've fallen on the ground, be sure they're not too crumbly. If they're still on the plants, be sure to ask before you pick!
    - Find a variety of shapes and sizes.

3. **Print your leaf.**
    - Put your leaf on the scrap paper, with the rough side of the leaf facing up.
    - Use your paintbrush to spread watercolors all over this side of the leaf. Don't use too much water if you want your colors to be bright!
    - Put the leaf on your large sheet of paper, paint side down.
    - Cover the leaf with a paper towel. Press down firmly, but be sure not to move the leaf. You don't want a blurry picture!
    - Remove the paper towel and the leaf, and admire your leaf print!

4. **Make the scene.**
    - Choose new leaves to print. Look for shapes that will add to your picture — a round leaf print can be someone's face, long ones can be legs.
    - You can use a leaf more than once, and you can paint it with more than one color. But be sure to clean your brush before you change color.

Activity Ten

5. **Let your leaves sing and dance.**
    - Use your markers to add details.
    - Will your biggest leaf be playing the guitar? Will your small one be the lead singer? And what is that funny dance they're all doing? Do you think I can learn it, too?

NIGHT VISION

Charles Burchfield, *Night of the Equinox*

Have you ever been afraid of the dark?

Charles Burchfield was.

When he was a child, he thought the nights were mysterious and even a little scary.

He was inspired by nature, much as Alma Thomas was, and he made it the center of his artwork, too.

This is one of Charles Burchfield's pictures. Do you think it's anything like Alma Thomas's? It's easy to see the differences. His picture is dark, and hers are bright.

In her paintings, only the colors and patterns of nature are shown. In his, we can see the trees, the clouds, and the sky. Alma Thomas concentrated on the cheerful things she saw. Burchfield chose stormier scenes.

But even though their art looks very different, in important ways Charles Burchfield and Alma Thomas were alike. They both pictured the forces in nature that matched their own feelings, and they both picked colors to express their moods.

How do you feel when it starts to get dark? Why don't you make a picture about it? Here's how:

1. **Get out these supplies:**
   - Heavy, white drawing paper (a large sheet)
   - crayons (bright colors)
   - watercolors (black or dark blue)
   - brush
   - jar of water
   - scrap paper

2. **Pick out a scene.**
   - Do you remember watching the sky get dark? You might have been looking from the door of a tent, from a car window, or even from your own bedroom.

3. **Picture your scene by day.**
   - With your crayons, draw your scene. But leave out the sun!
   - Color your picture again. Keep going over it until every place you've colored feels smooth and waxy.

4. **Make some liquid darkness!**
   - Put a little water (about 1" deep) in your glass.
   - Get your paintbrush wet, then put it in the blue or black watercolor.
   - Put the paintbrush in the water. Did the water turn dark?
   - Keep using your paintbrush to put paint in the water. You're making a color wash.
   - Test out your wash by painting a stripe on the scrap paper. Does it look light or dark? It should be very dark.

5. **Now picture your scene at night!**
   - Don't try to paint around your crayon drawing. Paint right over your whole daytime scene.
   - Make even strokes, but don't paint over the same areas twice.

6. **How does your scene make you feel now?**
   - Your daytime picture "jumps out" of the night. It's all still there. When it gets dark, things only look different!

Activity Eleven

CREATURE FEATURE

Have you ever made a shadow creature?

Sometimes, at night, I hold my hoof in front of a lamp and look for animals in the shadows I make on the wall. One painting looks a lot like those shadows, and it's a little frightening because I can't easily tell what it is.

And the other painting is scary because I **can** tell what it is!

Robert Motherwell called his painting **Monster**. Even though it doesn't really look like a monster, it **feels** like

Luis Jiménez, *Howl*

one. Robert Motherwell used brown and black to help make that feeling. In **Howl**, Luis Jiménez made the animal look more realistic. Do you think the bright colors make it look more friendly?

I think I'll make one of my shadow creatures out of paper. You can, too.

1. **Get out these supplies:**
   - drawing paper (a large sheet)
   - colored paper (a large sheet)
   - glue
   - markers or crayons

2. **Make your "shadow."**
   - Tear your colored paper into a few large pieces.
   - Don't try to make a certain shape. Just let them happen!
   - Pick the shapes you like best.
   - Glue the shapes on your drawing paper. Don't try to make a picture with them, and don't use too much glue!

Robert Motherwell, *Monster (for Charles Ives)*

3. **Look for the hidden creature.**
   - Turn your picture upside down and sideways. Do you see anything that reminds you of an animal? Look for eyes, ears, or a tail.

4. **Is your creature friendly or scary?**
   - Use your markers or crayons to help everyone see your creature.
   - Add as many details as you like.
   - Pick colors to let us know if we should pet your creature . . . or keep away!

Activity Twelve

DON'T THROW THAT AWAY!

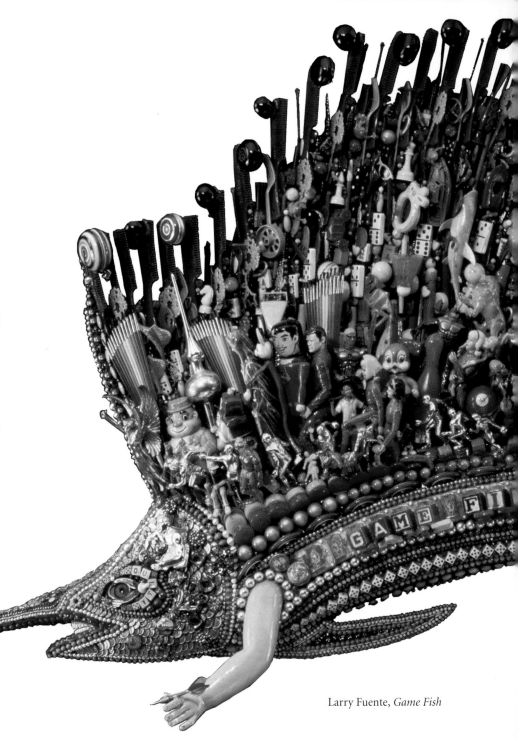

For most of the activities we've done so far, we've used supplies that are made especially for artists to use.

But some of the most interesting art in my museum was made with almost everything **except** ordinary art supplies!

Like this fish! Can you find anything **ordinary** about him?

After you see what these artists put in their artwork, you'll look at everything twice before you *decide* to throw it away.

I know **I do!** Some things never make it to the trash at all. **They turn up in art.**

Larry Fuente, *Game Fish*

That reminds me! I took some worn-down wheels off my skateboard when I was fixing it last week. They'd be great to use in my next project.

Now, let me think . . . I wonder where I put them?

JOSEPH CORNELL

(1903 – 1972)

Does anyone ever tease you about how many things you find and keep? Has anybody ever called you a "pack rat?"

Then you can imagine what Joseph Cornell's family might have said about **him**.

He lived in a small house on Utopia Parkway in Flushing, a suburb of New York City. He shared his house with his mother, his brother . . . and hundreds of file boxes and files full of fascinating stuff that inspired his artwork!

Cornell at work

Joseph Cornell, *Colombier*
(Dovecote #2)

He liked living near New York, and he delighted in exploring its streets and neighborhoods. Sometimes he wrote about the many unusual things he saw, but often he brought them home! Old books, records, photographs, movie films, theater programs—the shops he visited were full of these things. He collected whatever struck his fancy, no matter how old or ordinary it might look to someone else.

He called his collection a "diary journal, picture gallery, museum, and clearing house for dreams and visions," because it became an important part of his artwork.

Once, while wandering down a street, Cornell noticed some compasses in one store and boxes in another nearby. He wondered what these objects would look like together. "My work was a natural outcome of my love for the city," he said. He began making boxes for his collection, choosing objects that combine both materials and ideas. He found some surprising and marvelous combinations! We might not even notice something as ordinary as a postcard or a shell if we saw it by itself, but in one of Cornell's boxes, it suddenly seems very special and even a little mysterious. Cornell's boxes can make us think of all sorts of things . . . like magic games or secret rooms.

Joseph Cornell, *"Ideals Are Like Stars; You Will Not Succeed in Touching Them with Your Hands..." (Great Ideas of Western Man Series)*

Joseph Cornell was very shy and often sad, but he said that his boxes gave him "a world of complete happiness." An ideal world is sometimes called a *utopia.* Isn't it funny that Cornell make his "happy world" in a cluttered basement studio on Utopia Parkway?

Joseph Cornell, *Americana: Natural Philosophy* (detail)

COULD YOU GUESS THAT . . .

. . . Cornell's whole family liked the opera and the theater? Many people think his boxes look like stages — just waiting for the action to begin.

. . . Cornell loved a magician named Houdini? Houdini was a famous "escape artist." He could break loose from handcuffs, knotted ropes, and boxes that had been sealed shut. Many of Houdini's boxes had a secret — a trap door. Cornell's boxes seem to have secrets, too.

. . . after he grew up Cornell never left New York? He took pretend journeys when he made his boxes. He filled some of them with objects from other countries and gave them make-believe names in foreign languages. Some of his boxes are imaginary hotels in places he never visited, like southern France and North Africa.

. . . Cornell especially admired writer and nature lover Henry David Thoreau? Thoreau could have been talking about Cornell's art when he wrote, "The question is not what you look at, but what you see."

ACTIVITIES THAT USE EVERYDAY ITEMS IN NEW WAYS

"Everything is still the same as it was, but it's different."

—*Edward Wortz*

A TUNNEL BOX

Many of Joseph Cornell's boxes look like imaginary buildings from faraway places. Cut cardboard to make the walls, windows, and doors of a make-believe building of your own. Join them together so that we can enjoy visiting your building from the outside . . . and from the inside!

Here's how:

1. **Get out these supplies:**
   - pencil
   - scissors
   - glue
   - lightweight cardboard (about as thick as the cover of a paperback book)
   - colored paper
   - old cards and magazines
   - markers
   - odds and ends from **your** "pack rat" collection

Joseph Cornell, *Untitled (Medici Slot Machine Family, Caravaggio series)*

2. **Design your building.**
   - Think about the kind of building you want to make.
   - Look at magazine pictures of buildings for ideas.

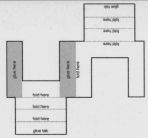

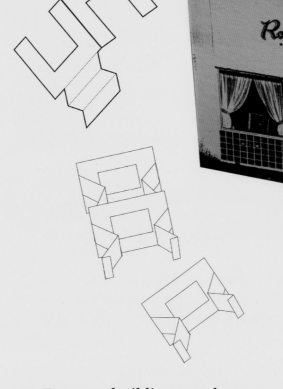

Activity Thirteen

3. Get ready!

- On one piece of cardboard, draw a shape like the one printed on this page. Make it as big as you want the walls of your make-believe building to be.
- Cut the shape out.

4. Start construction!

- Trace the shape on clean cardboard three more times. Cut these shapes out.

5. Build your walls.

- Fold each of your shapes in half along the fold line, and glue the two halves together.
- Now you have the walls of your building and doorways to see through.

6. Decorate the front of your building.

- Use markers, paper cutouts, scraps of foil or wood, stickers, etc. to make a front door, windows, and a roof.

7. Give yourself a "view" from the back door.

- Draw an interesting picture or cut one out of a magazine. Glue it over the opening in one of your shapes. This will be your back wall.

8. Put your building together.

- Fold all of the tabs back and forth along the fold lines, paper-fan style. (You can cut the tabs off the back wall of your building.) Arrange your walls in order, front to back.
- Glue the tabs of each wall to the wall behind it.
- Be sure to keep the sides of your walls lined up ... unless you want to have a crooked building!

9. Fill your rooms.

- What kind of building is it? To show us, add people, furniture, animals, and machines.
- Use magazine cutouts, markers, buttons, beads, or scraps of material to decorate the rooms of your building.
- Glue some things so that they cover a little of the inside doorways, so we can see them from the front door.

10. Peek inside!

- Look through the front door of your building and imagine what might be going on inside.
- You can make the rooms of your building bigger by gently pulling the front and back walls apart.

BURIED TREASURES

Lenore Tawney, *In Silence*

If you found a **treasure chest** in your neighborhood, what do you think would be in it?

It might be heaped with coins and jewels. Or it may only contain old things that nobody uses anymore.

But whatever you found, they would certainly have been **very special to the person who put them in** the chest. Why else would they have hidden them?

Lenore Tawney's artwork is like buried treasure. The things she collects — like shells and bottle corks — aren't valuable to most people, but they're very important to

her. She covers old papers with the things she collects. The papers give us clues about what she's found, and why she's kept it.

Make a hidden treasure of some things that are **important to you.**

Here's how:

1. **Get out these supplies:**
   - a small cardboard box
   - paint (Acrylic works best.)
   - paintbrush
   - stiff brush for glue
   - glue (water-based and clear-drying)
   - glass or jar of water
   - your "treasures," glitter, sequins, etc.

2. **Sort through your treasures.**
   - Choose some favorite objects from your "pack rat" collection of odds and ends.

3. **Try out your design.**
   - Paint your box a smooth, solid color.
   - While the paint dries, arrange your treasures on the table.
   - Your treasures don't need to line up. Scatter them around, and let them overlap!
   - Are you decorating only the top, or will you cover the sides, too?
   - Will your chest have a theme? Old postage stamps would be good on a letter box. Ribbons and beads make a jewelry box look great!

Activity Fourteen

4. **Cover your box.**
   - Use the stiff brush to spread a coat of glue evenly over the top and sides of your container. This is a time when it's okay to use a lot of glue!
   - Picking up your objects one at a time, set them into the wet glue.
   - Keep adding objects until your box is covered the way you planned. Sprinkle it with glitter or sequins.

5. **Turn it into a "chest."**
   - When your box is entirely dry, put on more glue! With your glue brush, spread a fairly thick and even coat of glue over everything.

6. **Watch for the hidden treasure!**
   - You won't be able to recognize anything on your box . . . for a while. But as the new layer of glue dries, it will become transparent.
   - Be patient! It might take a whole day to dry completely.
   - Now there are glittery treasures **on** your chest. What new treasures will you put **in** it?

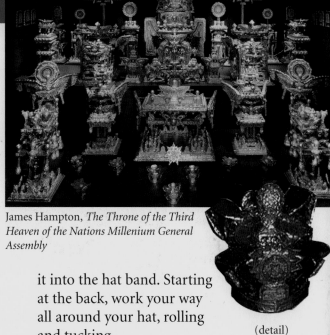

James Hampton, *The Throne of the Third Heaven of the Nations Millenium General Assembly*

(detail)

YESTERDAY'S NEWS

Underneath the museum, there's a **big garage**. Visitors don't usually go in it, but most people who work here do. It's where we park our cars, our bicycles, and of course our skateboards!

That's how most people use a garage. **They keep their machines and tools** in it, and even their trash cans — anything that might spoil the appearance of their "good" rooms.

James Hampton had different ideas for his garage. Instead of keeping his trash in it until collection day, **he filled it with objects other people threw out**. Used furniture, cardboard, light bulbs, old glasses — he put them all together and covered them with aluminum foil. He turned his garage into his very best room of all, a room fit for a king.

After I saw James Hampton's room, I took another look around our garage. In one corner was a bundle of old newspapers we save for recycling. I decided to try wearing them instead! You can, too.

1. **Get out these supplies.**
   - old newspaper
   - stapler
   - scissors
   - aluminum foil
   - tape or glue

2. **Cover your head.**
   - You need four thicknesses of newspaper to make a strong top for your hat.
   - Twist another sheet of newspaper into a rope that's long enough to fit around your head.

3. **Get a good fit!**
   - Ask someone to help you.
   - Set the four thickness of newspaper flat on top of your head.
   - Use the newspaper rope to make a hat band.
   - Put the band on top of the four sheets of newspaper. Let the flat edges hang down.
   - The hat band should feel snug. It will hold the top of your hat close to your head.
   - Get help stapling the ends of the newspaper rope together.
   - Roll the extra newspaper up and tuck it into the hat band. Starting at the back, work your way all around your hat, rolling and tucking.
   - When you get back to your starting point, push the last corner of the newspaper into the hat band. Make sure everything's tight!

4. **Make it fancy.**
   - Shiny silver tinfoil reminded James Hampton of kings and queens. Cut shapes out of tinfoil and tape or glue them onto your special hat!

5. **Wear the news.**
   - If anybody wants to know what's been going on the world, you can tap your head and tell them, "I've got all the facts right up here!"

Activity Fifteen

CAN YOU FIND THE SECRET MESSAGE?

With all the activities you've just done, you know that **almost anything can be used to make art!** Something might be old and ordinary, but by putting it into your artwork, you can make it change into something new and special.

This can happen with words and numbers, too.

Words and numbers are symbols. They are really only lines and shapes. You've learned to read and understand them, and you use them to tell your ideas.

You can change them, too. You can give them new meanings, or you can use them in a special new way.

And you can put them in your art!

Let's look at some artwork that uses words and numbers.

Do you think we'll be able to "read" what it's telling us?

(opposite)Jasper Johns, *Gray Alphabets* (detail)

(opposite, tablet)James Hampton,
The Throne of the Third Heaven of the Nations Millenium General Assembly (detail)

Robert Indiana, *Five*

ROBERT INDIANA

(b. 1928)

When the mailman has a letter for you, how does he know which house is yours?

If your backpack gets lost in the locker room, what shows that it belongs to you?

During the weekend, how does your best friend call you?

On a busy street, when do you know where it's safe to cross?

Street signs and house numbers, phone numbers and initials . . . you use important numbers and letters every-day. When your backpack gets lost in the locker room, a tag with your name on it tells everyone that it is yours. If your best friend has a secret to tell, she knows she can talk to you by dialing your telephone number. On a busy street, a crossing sign lets you know where it's safe to cross.

Words and numbers are important to Robert Indiana, too. He has turned them into a language of his own. He uses them to tell you what he's seen, what he's done, and what he thinks.

His artwork looks like road signs you might see along the highway. Sometimes they tell you about his life — the roads he's traveled and what's happened to him along the

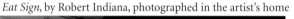

Robert Indiana in his studio

Eat Sign, by Robert Indiana, photographed in the artist's home

way. Sometimes they show what he enjoys, like poems and surprising stories. And sometimes they encourage us to do what he thinks we should — like "EAT" and "LOVE."

"Some people like to paint trees," he said. "I like to paint love. I find it more meaningful than painting trees."

Many people must agree with him.

Robert Indiana, *LOVE*

Look closely at the envelope addressed to "You". Does the stamp look familiar?

In 1973, the U.S. Postal Service put Robert Indiana's design on the very first "LOVE" stamp. Over three hundred and twenty million of these stamps were printed. Mail trucks carried letters with this small "LOVE" sign on them along highways all across the country.

Every time a letter with this stamp on it was delivered, Robert Indiana's message was being spread a little further!

COULD YOU GUESS THAT . . .

. . . **Robert Indiana was born in Indiana?** His parents' last name was "Clark." When he changed his name, Robert Indiana was finding another way to show how important words are to him.

. . . **a lot of his childhood was spent along busy highways?** Indiana remembers the neon signs and game machines from the roadside restaurants where his mother worked, and he puts their shapes into his artwork. He also likes to use the colors of his father's gasoline-company truck—red and green—with the blue and white of the sky and clouds behind it.

. . . **he found some old brass letter stencils when he moved his art studio into an old warehouse?** The stencils inspired him to use words in his paintings, and he likes painting letters that look as if they've been printed.

. . . **Robert Indiana thinks that most people never stop to think about how beautiful words and numbers are?** He said that he thinks his job as an artist is ". . . to make words and numbers very, very special."

ACTIVITIES THAT PLAY WITH LETTERS AND NUMBERS

"The words I use are everyday words and yet are not the same!"

—*Paul Claudel*

Robert Indiana isn't the only artist who uses words and numbers in a special way. **You can, too**.

See if you can use words and numbers to make a "picture" of who you are!

Robert Indiana, *The Figure Five*

A SIGN FOR YOUR BEDROOM DOOR

1. **Get out these supplies:**
    - pencil
    - scrap paper
    - colored paper
    - ruler
    - scissors
    - glue or glue stick
    - markers
    - number and letter stencils

2. **What words and numbers are important in your life?**
    - Fold your notebook paper in half. List special words on one side and special numbers on the other.
    - For ideas, think about your favorite books, your birthday, your friends' names, and the number of people in your family.
    - To make your design look more like a sign, use short words and numbers.

3. **Plan your sign.**
    - What shape will it be? What colors will you use? Where will the words and numbers go? Will they be different sizes?
    - You can cross some words and numbers off your list, and you can use other ones over and over again.

Robert Indiana's original *Love* maquette in cardboard and painted white

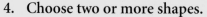

4. Choose two or more shapes.
- You can trace around a plate or other object that has the shape you need, or you can use your ruler to help you.

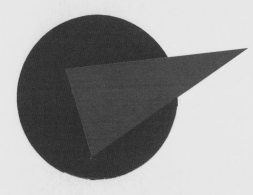

7. Add borders and outlines.
- Use marker or colored paper strips to make your shapes show up better and to cover pencil tracing lines.

6. Put the words and numbers on your sign.
- You can use stencils and markers, or you can cut them out of scraps of colored paper.
- Follow your plan!

5. Cut your shapes out and glue them together.
- You can put one shape on top of another one. They will make interesting spaces for your design.
- Don't use too much glue!

8. Hang your finished sign on your bedroom door!
- Ask an adult to help you.
- Can your friends and family "read" your message?

"HIDDEN" LETTERS

My best friend and I have a way of writing to each other that no one else can understand. It's our own **secret writing**, and we made it up ourselves.

Have you ever tried making up your own way of writing?

Chaz Bojórquez has. His painting looks very mysterious, but it's really a list of his friends' names!

He made up his own rules for making letters and punctuation marks. We can read what he writes if we learn the rules, too.

In this painting, Bojórquez made an "M" by putting an "X" on top of three "I"s, and a "Y" by drawing a triangle on top of a dot.

Can you find the names "Tony" and "Tommy" hidden in his painting? Do you think you could have found them without knowing his rules?

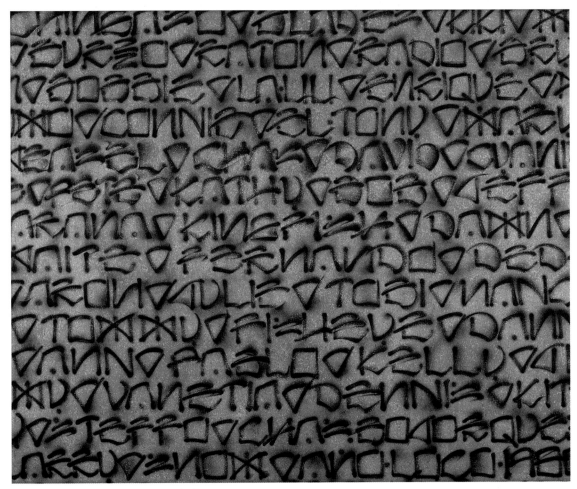

Charles "Chaz" Bojórquez, *Placa/Rollcall*

Here's some secret writing you can do!

1. **Get out these supplies:**
   - pencil
   - scrap paper
   - colored construction paper
   - clear-drying glue (A bottle with a pointed tip will make "writing" easier.)
   - colored chalk or pastels
   - tissue

2. **Plan your message.**
   - Choose one or two short words.
   - Think about what the letters of the alphabet look like. There are lots of different ways to make them. With your scrap paper, draw some bubble letters, or some fancy cursive ones.

- What direction will your letters go? They can go in circle, or in a diagonal line across the page. They can even be upside down!
- Make your letters big!

3. **Practice making lines with glue.**
   - Use a piece of scrap paper.
   - Pull the glue bottle away from the lines you're making. If you push the tip back through the glue, your lines will smear!
   - Squeeze the bottle just a little if you want thin lines. Squeeze harder for thick ones.

4. **"Hide" your message.**
   - Now you're ready for your real message.
   - Use the colored paper, and write your message in glue.
   - Keep your letters big!
   - Don't worry if you make mistakes or if the glue lines don't look like your pencil lines. Mistakes will help hide your message even more!
   - Let the glue dry.

5. **Give your message to your friend.**
   - Your message will still be a secret. It will look like a blank piece of paper with some old glue dripped on it.

6. **Help your friend find the hidden message!**
   - Color the whole paper with chalk or pastels.
   - Your glue lines made different shapes. You can use a different color for each one, or you can put different colors inside the same shape.
   - Color right up to — or even over — the glue lines!
   - Rub the chalk with tissue to help blend the colors.
   - Use the tissue to clean the chalk off the glue lines, so you can see the colored paper through them.
   - Can your friend read your secret writing?

Activity Seventeen

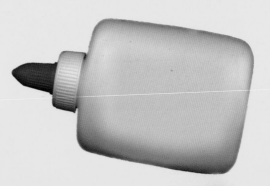

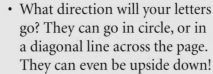

A REBUS

When I skate down the street, I ride past dozens of signs. But dozens more of them **zoom past** me !

Because **license plates are signs**, too.

The license plates on cars and trucks show who owns them. But they can do more than that. I like to look for **unusual** license plates — the ones with letters and numbers that fit together in surprising ways.

And I don't have to look very far! In his artwork, Mike Wilkins put **fifty-one** license plates together to surprise us this way. Can you sound out the words he made? They're from the Preamble of the Constitution of the United States of America.

Mike Wilkins turned the license plates into a word puzzle.

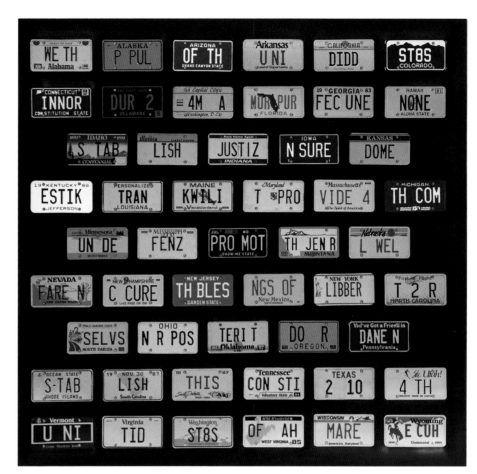

Mike Wilkins, *Preamble*

I had fun making a word puzzle of my own. In mine, I used pictures for some of the words. This sort of puzzle is called a **rebus.**

You can make a rebus, too! Here's how:

1. **Get out these supplies:**
   - notebook paper
   - pencil
   - drawing paper
   - markers
   - ink pad
   - rubber stamps (Use stamps you have or make your own. Foam insulation tape from the hardware store is easy to cut into shapes. Peel off the paper backing and stick each shape onto a small square of thick cardboard.)

2. **Write one or two sentences.**
   - Tell about something you did today, or something you'd like to do tomorrow.
   - Use your notebook paper to try out your ideas.

3. **Read your sentences out loud.**
   - Listen to how your words sound. Do you hear yourself saying the names of some numbers and letters as you read?
   - Circle the words (or parts of words) that sound like letters or numbers.

4. **Read your sentences again.**
   - Do some of your words sound like other things? Could simple pictures take their place? Circle these words and sounds, too.
   - You will make a word puzzle every place you've drawn a circle.

5. **Turn your sentences into a rebus.**
   - Copy the uncircled parts of your sentences onto a piece of drawing paper. Leave an empty space wherever you see a circle.
   - With your markers or rubber stamps, fill each blank space with a letter, number, or picture.

6. **Show your rebus to your friends.**
   - Can they read what you wrote?

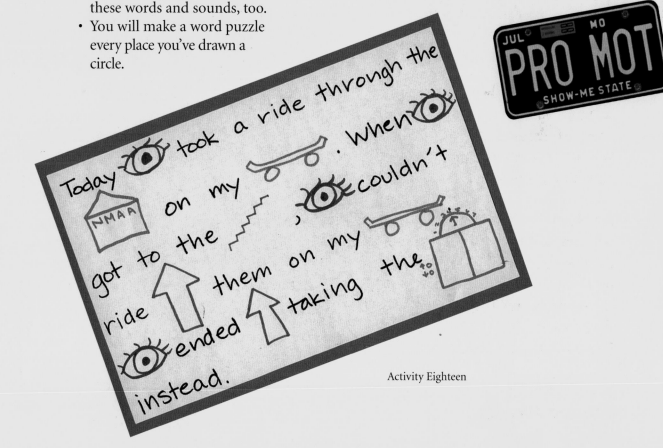

Activity Eighteen

Jasper Johns, *Souvenir*

DO YOU KNOW WHAT I THINK?

Or maybe I'll call it "Untitled," so you can make up your own name!

Do you make up **titles** for your pictures?

I've just painted a picture to show **why people should come to my museum**, but I'm having a hard time giving it a title. Will you help me think of one?

After I look at artwork in the museum, I always **read the labels** beside them.

Seeing the artists' names helps me remember who made my favorite art.

Larry Rivers,
Identification Manual

And, if there's a title, reading it helps me understand what the artists were thinking about while they were working.

Sometimes artists write their titles right on their artwork. And sometimes they write more of their ideas on it, too.

Maybe I should just call my picture **Museums Are Fun!** . . .

. . . because that's what I think.

SISTER GERTRUDE MORGAN

(1900 - 1980)

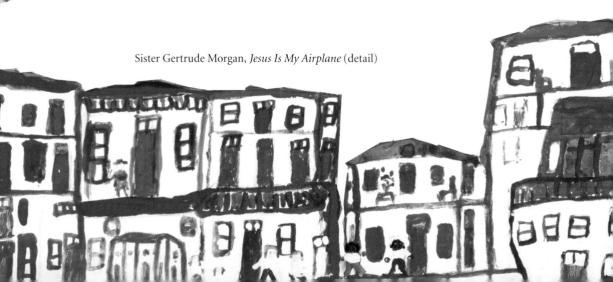

W hat would your school be like if all the **blackboards** disappeared?

What if the **bulletin boards** and the slide projectors were taken away, too?

Your teacher could still tell you about hurricanes during science class. And, during history period, your friend could still give an oral report about life in a colonial village. But if you couldn't **see** the things they were talking about, both of these classes might be a little confusing . . . and a little dull!

With a blackboard, your friend can point out the stores and houses on a map drawn in colored chalk. Then you can easily imagine what spending a day in a colonial village would be like. With a projector and bulletin board, your teacher can put up newspaper clippings and show slides of recent storms. Looking at them, you understand right away why learning about hurricanes is so important.

Sister Gertrude Morgan, *Jesus Is My Airplane* (detail)

Pictures and maps are called **visual aids.** There are different kinds of visual aids, but they all have the same purpose. They help us connect the words we hear to the pictures we see. They make learning new things less difficult and much more interesting.

Sister Gertrude Morgan wanted to help people learn, too. She believed that it was her job to teach everyone about her religion. To help people learn and remember, she did what **any** teacher does. She used visual aids! Instead of ordinary blackboards and bulletin boards, Sister Gertrude Morgan used her colorful artwork in her teaching. Sometimes she added lines from songs she wrote, and sometimes she made up poems, or copied parts of the **Bible.**

Sister Gertrude Morgan grew up in Alabama. She belonged to a religious group that played instruments, danced, and sang during their church services. Later, she moved to New Orleans and opened a small church of her own. She called it the "Everlasting Gospel Mission," and she became a **singing minister.**

When ministers teach the people in their church, they sometimes give a sort of speech called a **sermon.** Sister Morgan gave her sermons using her music and her art. "I guess my paintings spread the Word . . . ," she said.

Sister Gertrude Morgan

COULD YOU GUESS THAT . . .

. . . **when she was a child, Sister Gertrude Morgan didn't have art supplies?** She still wanted to draw, so she used sticks to make designs in the ground.

. . . **she made a record album of her church music?** She sang, played the guitar, and did the artwork on the cover, too!

. . . **teaching about her religion wasn't the only way Sister Gertrude Morgan tried to help people?** When she first moved to New Orleans, she and some other people built a chapel and opened a community service center to give food and shelter to those who needed it. She did this for twelve years, until a hurricane destroyed the center. (So you see how important learning about hurricanes can be!)

. . . **she painted and drew on anything she happened to have around?** Cardboard, styrofoam trays, blocks of wood, lamp shades, picture frames . . . even her guitar case is decorated!

ACTIVITIES THAT SHOW WHAT YOU THINK

"Painting is silent poetry, and poetry is painting that speaks."

—*Plutarch*

COVER-UPS

Sister Gertrude Morgan thought music was very important, and I do, too. But you'd never be able to guess what I thought about music by looking at my tapes and CD's. So I decided to make covers for my cases. Now it's easy to see what music I like best! This is what I did:

1. **Get out these supplies:**
   - pencils (#2 and colored)
   - scrap paper
   - lightweight posterboard or heavy drawing paper
   - scissors
   - old magazines
   - glue
   - stiff brush for glue
   - markers

Sister Gertrude Morgan, *Jesus Is My Airplane*

Activity Nineteen

2. **Try to "see" your music.**
   - Play your tape or CD again.
   - Do the sounds you're hearing remind you of anything? You may think of colors and shapes, or you may imagine a whole scene. Daydream while you listen.
   - Make a quick sketch of whatever you're "seeing."

3. **Make your cover.**
   - On the posterboard, use a pencil to trace around the pre-made cover from your tape or CD case.
   - Carefully cut our your new cover. Fold it like the old one so it will fit the case.
   - Copy the design from your quick sketch.
   - Expand your design to fill your cover. Don't forget the back and the hinge edge!

Activity Nineteen

4. Fill in your design.

- Will magazine cut-outs be good for some areas? You can cut out one whole picture or parts of several pictures.
- Spread the glue evenly before pasting the cut-outs to your cover.
- Try gluing things on top of each other. It's fun to mix things you'd never expect to see together!
- Use your markers and colored pencils to fill in any blank areas or to change the colors of the printed ones.

5. Give your new cover a new name.

- What did you picture in your mind when you listened to this music? When do you like to play it? Choose a name that tells something special about your tape or CD.
- Use markers or letters cut from magazines to put the name on your cover.
- Now everybody will know what **you** think!

Sister Gertrude Morgan

Sister Gertrude Morgan, *Let's Make a Record*

FITS TO A "T"!

Art can show us a lot about what an artist thinks is important. For Sister Gertrude Morgan, nothing meant more to her than her **religious beliefs,** so that's what she chose to paint about. Sam Gilliam wanted to tell us some of his ideas about

Sam Gilliam, *(Equal Employment Opportunity Is the Law, portfolio) T-shirt*

politics. If he walked by wearing a T-shirt like this one, you'd know right away how he felt about being fair.

The words and pictures on T-shirts can be like **walking advertisements**. What message do you want to spread? Let your T-shirt do it for you!

Here's how:

1. **Ask an adult for help.**
   - You'll need some special materials for this project.
   - Don't use the iron or the clothes dryer without permission!

2. **Get out these supplies:**
   - scrap paper
   - pencil
   - a sheet of sandpaper (medium coarseness, 6" x 8")
   - crayons
   - iron
   - pressing cloth
   - scrap paper or cardboard
   - a clean, solid-color T-shirt (100% cotton is best.)

3. **What do you want to say to the world?**
   - What do **you** think is important? Do you have a favorite sports team? Do you want to let people know about a place you've visited, a club you've joined, or a hobby you've started? What would you like people to learn about you?
   - Use your pencil and scrap paper to draw your design.

4. **Make an iron-on.**
   - With your crayons, copy your design onto the sandpaper.
   - Anything you print with an iron-on is reversed. So if you have words in your design, make the letters backwards and write the sentences from end to beginning. (If you hold your writing up to a mirror, you'll see how this looks.) If your words are wrong on the sandpaper, they'll turn out right on your T-shirt!
   - Go over your design again. The more crayon you use now, the darker your design will be when you print it.

5. **Print your T-shirt.**
   - Put a piece of cardboard or several sheets of scrap paper inside your T-shirt. This will keep your design from soaking through to the back.
   - Place the sandpaper, crayoned side down, where you want it to be on your shirt.
   - Ask an adult to help you. Set your iron for a medium-high heat, and put the pressing cloth over the sandpaper. Hold the hot iron firmly for about a minute on each area of your design. You can peek under the sandpaper to check your print, but be careful not to move the sandpaper!
   - A few minutes in the clothes dryer, at the permanent-press temperature setting, will make your design colorfast.

6. **Spread the word.**
   - Enjoy wearing your T-shirt. If your friends want one, too, all you have to do is go over your sandpaper design with crayon again.

Activity Twenty

A PICTURE POEM

Because I write in English, my words usually go from left to right and from the top of a page to the bottom.

But our **words make shapes**, too.

For instance,

        the words I just wrote look a
          little like a rectangle, but
            I could easily make
               them into a
                triangle,
                  like
                   th
                    i
                    s
                    !

Making your words fill up shapes can be one more way of telling us what you're saying.

Because when you make your writing form shapes, we can **see** what you're writing about before we read it!

This is what **Ben Shahn** was doing when he made this print.

He's written "Channel 13" over and over again. Thirteen is the number of a public television station that's part of an educational network.

What shape do Ben Shahn's words make?

Does the shape help you understand what he thinks about television?

I made a picture poem that tells — and shows — something **I** like.

Ben Shahn, *Owl No. 2* (detail)

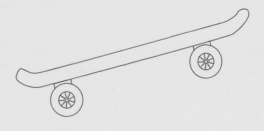

2. Write a poem.

- Think of something you like. Do you have a favorite sport or hobby? Is bug-collecting interesting to you? What else do you enjoy?
- Pick one of these things to write about. Tell what you like about it.
- Your poem doesn't have to be long. It doesn't even have to rhyme!

Here's how you can, too:

1. Get out these supplies:

- scrap paper
- pencil
- drawing paper (two sheets)
- colored pens
- colored paper
- glue

3. Draw a matching shape.

- What shape fits the words in your poem? Keep it simple.
- Using pencil, draw a large outline of your shape on one sheet of paper.
- Using pen, go over the pencil outline.

5. Display your work!

- Glue your poem to a sheet of colored paper. A little glue in each corner will be enough!
- Hold up your poem. Do your words make a shape? Does your poem **show** us what it **tells** us?

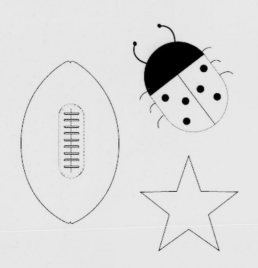

4. Copy your poem.

- Put the second piece of paper over the first one. Does the shape you drew show through? You'll use it as a guide. **Don't** draw the shape on the top sheet.
- With a pencil, copy your poem on the top sheet. Pay attention to your outline drawing, and make sure your words fill the shape.
- Go over your words with colored pens.

Activity Twenty-One

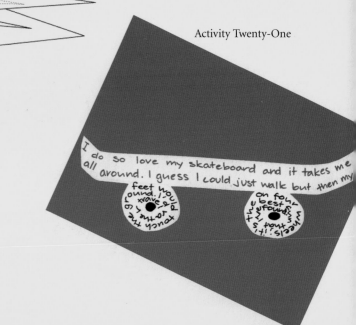

I do so love my skateboard and it takes me all around. I guess I could just walk but then my feet would...

Unidentified Artist, *Memory High-Button Shoe*

SURPRISE US!

The artwork in the last section is interesting because of the **ideas** the artist showed us.

But some artwork is interesting just because of the materials the artist used.

Can you think back to the beginning of this book, when we first started out together?

I told you about my artwork, and how, even though I get good ideas from my favorite artists, **the things I make never look the way theirs do.**

Sometimes they don't even look the way I thought they would! That makes me happy, because I like surprises.

Here are some **artists who like surprises,** too.

What are they showing us that you've never seen before?

What will you put in your artwork that you've never tried before?

Surprise us!

Robert Hudson, *After Wood*

ROBERT RAUSCHENBERG
(b. 1925)

Robert Rauschenberg thinks that **anything** — cardboard, tires, light bulbs, photographs, old clothes, even dirt — **can be used to make art.**

If people can paint on canvas, why can't they paint on the canvas of an old sneaker? he wondered. And do they have to use paint at all? He was curious about this, and so he began **experimenting with different materials,** to see how they would work.

Many people have noticed the joy and energy in Rauschenberg's artwork. He says it comes from this kind of curiosity. He is curious about **everything!**

He is curious about what other artists are doing. He often works with friends who are artists and writers.

He is **curious about technology.** Rauschenberg was especially excited about new methods of printing and photography — even X-rays. He asked master craftsmen to help him use these technologies in his artwork.

Rauschenberg in his Front Street Studio, 1958

Robert Rauschenberg, *Reservoir*

He is curious about the world. Rauschenberg likes to put things he finds — like clocks and wheels — in his paintings. "I think a painting is more like the real world if it's made out of the real world," he said.

This picture of an animal feed bag on the next page is made out of part of the "real world." It **looks** real, too, when you first see it.

But what has Rauschenberg added that you'd never see on any pet food shelf? How has he surprised us?

COULD YOU GUESS THAT . . .

. . . **Robert Rauschenberg's work was in the nation's bicentennial exhibition right here at the National Museum of American Art?** One of the Museum's curators thought that Rauschenberg was perfect for the exhibition because he was both a great artist and a great citizen.

. . . **he thought of himself as an artist-reporter?** He said his job was to be a witness to his time in history.

. . . **clocks were especially interesting to him?** He liked thinking about all the different ways we measure time.

. . . **Robert Rauschenberg is dyslexic?** Reading was very difficult for him in school — sometimes he saw words backwards, upside-down, or even double.

. . . **he never saw a work of art until he was almost twenty years old?** When he was growing up, no one in his house even talked about art.

. . . **he grew up in Port Arthur, Texas?** Some people think his artwork is a little like a Texas "tall tale."

. . . **When people see Rauschenberg's art, they sometimes ask, "Is he making a joke?"** What do you think?

ACTIVITIES THAT SURPRISE US

"I am only a public entertainer who has understood his time."

—*Pablo Picasso*

Robert Rauschenberg, *The Chow Series: Hog Chow*

CRITTER CHOW

I wonder if Robert Rauschenberg has make-believe pets?

They don't allow real animals in the Museum, and I don't have any stuffed ones. Sometimes I pretend that the other sculptures in the museum are my pets. When mealtime comes around, I really have to use my imagination to decide what these friends might want to eat. I've made some boxes and bags for their funny snacks.

Why don't you make a special container for your pets' food?
Here's how:

1. **Get out these supplies:**
   - scrap paper
   - pencil
   - an empty food container
   - construction paper
   - scissors
   - glue or tape
   - markers

2. **Decide who you'll be feeding, and what you'll give them.**
   - Does your dog or cat have a favorite snack? You can use your container to store treats for a real animal, or your snacks can be imaginary, too!
   - The ducks at the lake and the birds in your yard are always hungry!
   - If they were real, what sort of treats would your stuffed animals like?
   - What do you think an imaginary animal like the jackalope might eat?

3. Design your container.

- Use your pencil and scrap paper to sketch your ideas.
- Will your container have pictures of your pet? A cartoon bubble can show what he thinks of his treat!
- What will you name your special brand of pet food?

4. Make your "critter chow."

- Use your empty food container as a guide.
- With your pencil, trace all the shapes that make your container onto your construction paper. Don't leave out the top and bottom!
- Use your pencil and markers to copy your design from the scrap paper to the construction paper.
- Cut out the shapes and tape or glue them to the matching spaces on your container.

5. Feed your pet!

Activity Twenty-Two

SNEAKER CREATURE

"Mr. Imagination" is certainly a good name for this artist.
Who would ever think of making a bunch of old paintbrushes into such an amazing creature?

Look at the pictures on this page. Many artists use their imaginations to change everyday objects into surprising sculptures. I'm going to use an old sneaker to make a funny creature of my own. Why don't you work along with me? We can be "The Imagination Team!"

Mr. Imagination,
Portrait Head, Paintbrush Tree (detail)

2. **Get out these supplies:**
   - paint (Acrylic paint works best.)
   - paintbrush
   - markers
   - fabric scraps, yarn, buttons, and other "treasures"
   - scissors
   - glue

3. **Clean up your creature.**
   - Paint the whole shoe.
   - Let this coat of paint dry completely.

4. **Give him an interesting personality.**
   - Turn your shoe in different directions. Where are the eyes? Will the shoelaces be part of his body? Is that the tongue of the shoe, or is it the mouth of your creature?
   - Is your creature gentle or fierce? Is he usually sleepy, or is he always full of energy? We should be able to tell by expression on his face.
   - Yarn hair and button eyes can make your animal seem to "come alive." What else could you glue onto your sneaker to add more details to your creature? Use your paint and markers, too!

1. **Ask an adult for help.**
   - Which shoes have been outgrown or worn out? They're the ones to use for this project!

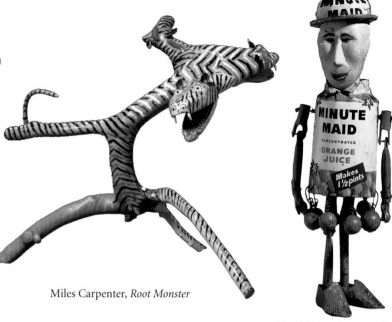

Miles Carpenter, *Root Monster*

Unidentified Artist, *Articulate Figure of Bing Crosby*

5. **Let your creature "sneak up" on your friends!**

Activity Twenty-Three

A BOTTLECAP SNAKE

When you first met me, I asked you if you'd ever seen a bottlecap giraffe before.

Now let me **introduce** you to my cousin!

You can make a bottle cap animal of your own!

Here's how:

1. Ask an adult for help:

- Could they please save the caps from their empty bottles for you? You can use pry-off or twist-off caps. The more caps you save, the longer your snake can be!
- Don't use a hammer or nails without permission.
- Find a good place to work. You don't want nail holes in anything but the bottle caps!

2. Get out these supplies:

- wire
- metal bottle caps
- hammer
- strong nails
- self-hardening clay
- poster paint and brushes, or colored markers
- construction paper scraps
- scissors
- glue
- old buttons

3. Give your snake a head:

- Make a 2" loop at one end of your wire. (You may need an adult's help.)
- Cover the loop with a ball of clay. Squeeze it and shape it to make the head of your snake.
- Cut out a construction paper tongue and stick it into the mouth-end of your snake's head.
- When the clay dries, use your markers or paint to make a face.

Activity
Twenty-Four

4. Make the snakeskin scales.

- Use the hammer and nails to make a hole in the center of each bottle cap. (You will need an adult's help now.)
- Try not to flatten the edges of the bottle caps.

5. String it up.

- Thread the straight end of the wire through the bottle cap holes.
- Make sure the tops of your bottle caps are all facing in the same direction.
- Leave enough wire at the end for a tail!

6. Add a tail.

- String the buttons onto the wire. Make a small loop in the end to hold them in place.
- Help your snake slither around. Listen for the rattle! Who will you surprise with **this?**

Unidentified Artist,
Sturgeon Decoy

CAPPY SAYS GOODBYE!

This is the end of **our art trip together**, but it doesn't have to be the end of yours.

Where you go from here is up to you. I'll bet you have lots of ideas for things you want to see and do in art.

But now it's getting late. More people have come to the museum, and they're all probably wondering where I am. So I'd better get back fast.

Thank heavens for my skateboard!

LIST OF ILLUSTRATIONS

Page 3: Alma Thomas (1891–1978). *Elysian Fields*, 1973. Acrylic on canvas, 76.5 x 107.2 cm (30 1/8 x 42 1/8 in.). Bequest of Alma W. Thomas. **Page 4:** Unidentified Artist. *Bottlecap Giraffe* (detail), completed after 1966. Carved and painted wood, bottlecaps, rubber, glass, animal hair, and fur, 184.2 x 137.2 x 44.5 cm (72 1/2 x 54 x 17 1/2 in.). Gift of Herbert Waide Hemphill, Jr., and museum purchase made possible by Ralph Cross Johnson. **Page 5:** Unidentified Artist, *Bottlecap Lion*, completed after 1966. Carved and painted wood, bottlecaps, flashcube, fiberboard, and plastic, 74.3 x 125.8 x 38.1 cm (29 1/4 x 49 1/2 x 15 in.). Gift of Herbert Waide Hemphill, Jr. and museum purchase made possible by Ralph Cross Johnson. **Page 8:** Alvan Fisher (1792–1863). *A General View of the Falls of Niagara* (detail), 1820. Oil on canvas, 87.2 x 122.3 cm (34 3/8 x 48 1/4 in.). Museum purchase. **Page 10:** Larry Yáñez (b. 1949). *Cocina Jaiteca, from the National Chicano Screenprint Taller, 1988–1989*, 1988. Serigraph on paper, 102.2 x 65.4 cm (40 1/4 x 25 3/4 in.). Gift of the Wight Art Gallery, University of California at Los Angeles. © 1988, Self-Help Graphics and Art, Inc. **Page 14:** Joseph Yoakum (1886–1972). *Art Linkletter's Ranch near Darwin, Australia*, June 2, 1966. Crayon, pastel, and ballpoint pen on paper, 30.2 x 45.4 cm

(11 7/8 x 17 7/8 in.). Gift of Herbert Waide Hemphill, Jr., and museum purchase made possible by Ralph Cross Johnson. **Page 15:** Barbara Bosworth (b. 1953). *Niagara Falls*, 1990. Gelatin silver print on paper, 19.5 x 24.4 cm (7 11/16 x 19 5/8 in.). Gift of the Consolidated Natural Gas Company Foundation. © 1986 by Barbara Bosworth; John Henry Twachtman (1853–1902). *Niagara Falls*, ca. 1894. Oil on canvas, 76.1 x 63.7 cm (30 x 25 1/8 in.). Gift of John Gellatly; George Inness (USA 1825–1894 Scotland). *Niagara Falls*, 1885. Oil on wood, 40.2 x 60.9 cm (15 7/8 x 24 in.). Gift of John Gellatly. **Page 16:** Jacob Lawrence (b. 1917). *Men Exist for the Sake of One Another. Teach Them Then or Bear with Them (from the Great Ideas of Western Man Series)*, 1958. Oil on prepared fiberboard: masonite, 52.6 x 42.4 cm (20 3/4 x 16 3/4 in.). Gift of the Container Corporation of America. **Page 18:** Velino Shije Herrera (1902–1973). *Story Teller* (detail), ca. 1925–1935. Gouache and pencil on paperboard, 25.6 x 38.2 cm (10 1/16 x 15 1/16 in.). Corbin-Henderson Collection. Gift of Alice H. Rossin. **Page 19:** Awa Tsireh (ca. 1895–ca. 1955). *Black Mountain Lion and Black Fox* (details), ca. 1925–1930. Watercolor, ink, and pencil on paper, 28.5 x 36.2 cm (11 1/4 x 14 1/4 in.). Corbin-Henderson Collection. Gift of Alice H. Rossin. **Page 22:** Residents of Bourbon

County, Kentucky (n.d.). *Fan Quilt, Mt. Carmel*, January 16, 1893. Embroidered, appliquéd, and pieced cotton, wool, velvet, and silk, with ribbon, paint, and chromolithographic decals, 215.9 x 183.5 cm (85 x 72 1/4 in.). Gift of Herbert Waide Hemphill, Jr., and museum purchase made possible by Ralph Cross Johnson. **Page 23:** Jack Earl (b. 1934). *Dear Fay . . .*, 1984. Painted ceramic, 52.7 x 52.1 x 44.5 cm (20 3/4 x 20 1/2 x 17 1/2 in.). Gift of KPMG Peat Marwick; Roger Shimomura (b. 1939). *Diary: December 12, 1941*, 1941. Acrylic on canvas, 152.4 x 127.6 cm (50 1/4 x 60 in.). Gift of the artist. **Page 24:** Gus Foster (b. 1940). *Cut Wheat*, 1988. Type-C print on paper mounted on paper, 45.7 x 218.7 cm (18 x 86 1/8 in.). Gift of the Consolidated Natural Gas Company Foundation. © 1988 by Gus Foster. Thomas Hart Benton (1889–1975). *Wheat* (detail), 1967. Oil on wood, 50.8 x 53.3 cm (20 x 21 in.). Gift of Mr. and Mrs. James A. Mitchell and museum purchase. **Page 27:** Georgia O'Keeffe (1887–1986). *Only One*, 1959. Oil on canvas, 91.5 x 76.4 cm (36 x 30 1/8 in.). Gift of S.C. Johnson & Son, Inc. **Page 28:** Georgia O'Keeffe (1887–1986). *Yellow Calla*, 1926. Oil on fiberboard, 22.9 x 32.4 cm (9 3/8 x 12 3/4 in.). Gift of the Woodward Foundation. **Page 30:** Alfredo Arreguín (b. Mexico 1935). *Sueño (Dream: Eve Before Adam)* (detail),

1992. Oil on canvas, three panels: each 182.9 x 121.9 cm (72 x 48 in.). Museum purchase through the Luisita L. and Franz H. Denghausen Endowment and the Smithsonian Collections Acquisition Program. **Page 31:** Gus Foster (b. 1940). *Cut Wheat*, 1988. Type-C print on paper mounted on paper, 45.7 x 218.7 cm (18 x 86 1/8 in.). Gift of the Consolidated Natural Gas Company Foundation. © 1988 by Gus Foster; Joe Jones (1909–1963). *Men and Wheat (mural study, Seneca, Kansas Post Office)*, 1939. Oil on canvas, 39.3 x 89.5 cm (15 1/2 x 35 1/4 in.). Transfer from the U.S. Department of the Interior, National Park Service. Thomas Hart Benton (1889–1975). *Wheat*, 1967. Oil on wood, 50.8 x 53.3 cm (20 x 21 in.). Gift of Mr. and Mrs. James A. Mitchell and museum purchase; **Pages 32–33:** Gene Davis (1920–1985). *Raspberry Icicle*, 1967. Synthetic polymer: acrylic on fabric: canvas, 294.6 x 558.4 cm (116 x 219 5/8 in.). Museum purchase. **Page 34:** Alma Thomas (1891–1978). *The Eclipse*, 1970. Acrylic on canvas, 57.5 x 126.5 cm (62 x 49 3/4 in.). Gift of Alma W. Thomas. The Smithsonian Institution makes no representation as to copyright status of this work. **Page 35:** Alma Thomas (1891–1978). *Autumn Leaves Fluttering in the Breeze*, 1973. Acrylic on canvas 101.5 x 127 cm (40 x 50 in.). Bequest of Alma W. Thomas. **Page 36:** Alma Thomas (1891–1978). *Red Azaleas Singing and Dancing Rock and Roll Music* (detail), 1976. Acrylic on canvas, 183.5 x 344.2 cm (72 1/4 x 156

3/4 in.). Bequest of Alma W. Thomas. **Page 38:** Charles Burchfield (1863–1967). *Night of the Equinox*, 1917–1955. Watercolor, brush and ink, gouache, and charcoal on paper mounted on paperboard, 102 x 132.5 cm (40 1/8 x 52 3/16 in.). Gift of the Sara Roby Foundation. **Page 39:** Luis Jiménez (b. 1940). *Howl*, 1977. Color lithograph, 91.9 x 66.3 cm (36 3/16 x 26 1/8 in.). Gift of the artist; Robert Motherwell (1915–1991). *Monster (for Charles Ives)*, 1959. Oil on canvas, 198.8 x 300.4 cm (78 1/4 x 118 1/4 in.). Gift of S.C. Johnson & Son, Inc. **Pages 40–41:** Larry Fuente (b. 1947). *Game Fish*, 1988. 130.8 x 285.6 x 27.3 cm (51 1/2 x 112 1/2 x 10 3/4 in.). Gift of the James Renwick Alliance and museum purchase through the Smithsonian Collections Acquisition Program. © 1988 by Larry Fuente. **Page 42:** Joseph Cornell (1903–1972). *Colombier (Dovecote #2)*, ca. 1950. Tempera and ink on newsprint, wood, and glass, 48.4 x 32.7 x 10.2 cm (19 1/16 x 12 7/8 x 4 in.). Gift of Mr. and Mrs. John A. Benton. **Page 43:** Joseph Cornell (1903–1972). *"Ideals Are Like Stars; You Will Not Succeed in Touching Them with Your Hands..." (Great Ideas of Western Man Series)*, ca. 1957–1958. Painted and stained wood, glass, shells, driftwood, and paper, 44.2 x 32.7 x 8.9 cm (17 3/8 x 12 7/8 x 3 1/2 in.). Gift of the Container Corporation of America; Joseph Cornell (1903–1972). *Americana: Natural Philosophy (What Makes the Weather?)* (detail), ca. 1955. Masonite, paper, paint, colored pencil, graphite, and ink, 30.5 x

22.8 cm (12 x 9 in.). Gift of Robert Lehrman in honor of Lynda Roscoe Hartigan.© 1995, The Joseph and Robert Cornell Memorial Foundation. **Page 44:** Joseph Cornell (1903–1972). *Untitled (Medici Slot Machine Family, Caravaggio series)*, Unfinished variant, ca. 1948–1949. Wood box construction with glass, photo-mechanical reproductions, and paint, 59.7 x 41.3 x 11.2 cm (23 1/4 x 16 1/4 x 4 7/16 in.). Gift of Mr. and Mrs. John A. Benton. **Page 46:** Lenore Tawney (b. 1907). *In Silence*, 1968. Paper, ink, shell, and wood, 18.8 x 22.3 x 2.8 cm (7 3/8 x 8 3/4 x 1 1/8 in.). Gift of KPMG Peat Marwick. © 1970 by Lenore G. Tawney. **Page 47:** James Hampton (1909–1964). *The Throne of the Third Heaven of the Nations Millenium General Assembly*, ca. 1950–64. Gold and silver aluminum foil, colored kraft paper, and plastic sheets over wood furniture, paperboard, and glass; 180 pieces in overall configuration, 8.2 x 4.4 m (10 1/2 x 27 x 14 1/2 ft.). Gift of anonymous donors. **Page 48:** James Hampton (1909–1964). *The Throne of the Third Heaven of the Nations Millenium General Assembly* (detail); Jasper Johns (b. 1930). *Gray Alphabets*, 1968. Color lithograph on paper, 29.5 x 86.4 cm (51 x 34 in.). Transfer from the National Endowment for the Arts. © 1968 Jasper Johns. **Page 49:** Robert Indiana (b. 1928). *Five*, 1984. Painted wood ceiling beam, wood dowel, wood block, and metal wheels, 175.6 x 67.9 x 47 cm. (69 1/8 x 26 3/4 x 18 1/2 in.). Gift of the artist. © 1984 by Robert Indiana.

Page 51: Robert Indiana (b. 1928). *LOVE*, 1973. Serigraph, 76.2 x 76.2 cm (30 x 30 in.). Gift of David Lloyd Kreeger. © 1973 by Robert Indiana. **Page 52:** Robert Indiana (b. 1928). *The Figure Five*, 1963. Oil on canvas, 152.4 x 127 x 1.3 cm (60 x 50 1/2 in.). Museum purchase. © 1963 by Robert Indiana. **Page 54:** Charles "Chaz" Bojórquez (b. 1949). *Placa/Rollcall*, 1980. Acrylic on canvas, 173.4 x 211 cm (68 1/4 x 83 1/8 in.). Gift of the artist. **Page 56:** Mike Wilkins (n.d.). *Preamble*, 1987. Painted metal, vinyl, and wood, 243.8 x 243.8 cm (96 x 96 in.). Gift of the Nissan Motor Corporation in U.S.A. **Page 58:** Jasper Johns (b. 1930). *Souvenir*, 1970. Color lithograph on paper, 78.7 x 57.8 cm (31 x 22 3/4 in.). Gift of Robert H. Klayman. © 1970 Jasper Johns. **Page 59:** Larry Rivers (b. 1923). *Identification Manual*, 1964. Mixed media and collage on fiberboard, 187 x 214.3 x 48.3 cm (73 5/8 x 84 3/8 x 19 in.). Gift of the Container Corporation of America. **Pages 60–61 (detail), 62:** Sister Gertrude Morgan (1900–1980). *Jesus Is My Airplane*, ca. 1970. Tempera, ballpoint pen, ink and pencil on paper, 45.7 x 67 cm (18 x 26 3/8 in.). Gift of Herbert Waide Hemphill, Jr., and museum purchase made possible by Ralph Cross Johnson. **Page 63:** Sister Gertrude Morgan (1900–1980). *Let's Make a Record*, ca. 1978. Album cover: tempera, acrylic, and pencil on paperboard, 31.4 x 31.8 cm (12 3/8 x 12 1/2 in.); Album: ceramic, 30.2 cm diameter (11 7/8 in.). Gift of Chuck and Jan Rosenak. **Page 64:** Sam Gilliam (b. 1933). *(Equal Employment Opportunity Is the Law, portfolio) T shirt*, 1973. Serigraph on paper, 55.8 x 76.2 cm (22 x 30 in.). Gift of the BLK Group, Inc. **Page 66–67:** Ben Shahn (Lithuania 1898–1969 USA). *Owl No. 2* (detail), 1968. Lithograph, 67 x 51.7 cm (26 3/8 x 20 3/8 in.). Gift of Atelier Mourlot Ltd. **Page 68:** Unidentified Artist. *Memory High-Button Shoes*, early 20th century. Masonite with composition dough embedded with metal, plastic, glass, and wood, 39.1 x 31.4 x 6.1 cm (15 1/2 x 12 3/8 x 2 3/8 in.). Gift of Herbert Waide Hemphill, Jr., and museum purchase made possible by Ralph Cross Johnson. **Page 69:** Robert Hudson (b. 1938). *After Wood*, 1990. Painted steel, 86.4 x 59.7 x 58.2 cm (34 x 23 1/2 x 22 7/8 in.). Gift of Mrs. Jaquelin Hume. **Page 71:** Robert Rauschenberg (b. 1925). *Reservoir*, 1961. Oil, wood, graphite, fabric, metal, and rubber on canvas, 217.2 x 158.7 x 37.4 cm (85 1/2 x 62 1/2 x 14 3/4 in.). Gift of S.C. Johnson & Son, Inc. **Page 72:** Robert Rauschenberg (b. 1925). *The Chow Series, Hog Chow*, 1977. Serigraph and stitching on paper, 122.2 x 92.1 cm (48 1/8 x 36 5/16 in.). Gift of Edward Dunay. © 1977 Robert Rauschenberg. **Page 74:** Mr. Imagination (b. 1948). *Portrait Head, Paintbrush Tree*, (detail) 1991. Bottlecaps, paintbrushes, and paint on wood, 165.4 x 57.8 x 47.6 cm (65 1/8 x 22 3/4 x 18 3/4 in.). Museum purchase; Miles Carpenter (1889–1985). *Root Monster*, 1968. Carved and painted tree roots, rubber, metal, and string, 57.5 x 72.7 x 71.6 cm (22 5/8 x 28 5/8 x 28 1/4 in.). Gift of Herbert Waide Hemphill, Jr., and museum purchase made possible by Ralph Cross Johnson; Unidentified Artist. *Articulated Figure of Bing Crosby*, ca. 1950s. Minute Maid orange juice can, carved and painted wood, and turned iron, 26.7 x 9 x 7 cm (10 1/2 x 3 1/2 x 2 3/4 in.). Gift of Herbert Waide Hemphill, Jr., and museum purchase made possible by Ralph Cross Johnson. **Page 75:** Unidentified Artist. *Sturgeon Decoy*, ca. 1950s. Carved and painted wood with bottlecaps, galvanized iron, and plastic, 15.2 x 66.7 x 16.3 cm (6 x 26 1/4 x 6 1/2 in.). Gift of Herbert Waide Hemphill, Jr., and museum purchase made possible by Ralph Cross Johnson. The Smithsonian Institution makes no representation as to copyright status of this work.

PHOTO CREDITS

Lynn-Steven Engelke is a visual artist and teacher. She has exhibited nationally and has taught art for over 15 years and at every level, pre-Kindergarten through college. Believing that children need to see themselves as the creators, she chooses art activities that foster independent learning with supplies readily available.